# SEX DIFFERENCE EXPLAINED:

From DNA to Society – Purging Gene Copy Errors

by Steve Moxon

# SEX DIFFERENCE EXPLAINED:

From DNA to Society – Purging Gene Copy Errors

By: Steve Moxon

Copyright: Steve Moxon

Broomhill, Sheffield, UK

Contact: stevemoxon3@talktalk.net

# FOREWORD

*New Male Studies (NMS) Publishing* inaugurates its monograph series with this essay by British independent researcher, Steve Moxon. It is in the interests of stimulating lively discussion that we present this very bold and lively text, which is, whatever may eventually be the verdict about its conclusions, grounded in solid science.

The Australian Institute of Men's Health and Studies (AIMHS), which sponsors the journal and monograph series, has established a reputation for not holding back on grounds of perhaps offending political correctness. As in the articles published in our journal, here in Mr Moxon's essay, some very strong views are offered. We leave it to the reader to take those views seriously and judge whether the science underlying them justifies Mr Moxon's conclusions, and their impli-cations for practice and policy-making.

The Australian Institute of Men's Health and Studies and *New Male Studies (NMS) Publiushing* are pleased to make this essay available. The views expressed by the author are not necessarily those of the editorial and supporting boards' members. We would like to acknowledge the gener-ous participation of an outside reader who raised important questions for clarification of earlier drafts of the essay.

**Miles Groth**
Editor, New Male Studies (NMS) Publishing
New York, NY
November 2016

# TABLE OF CONTENTS

FOREWORD ............................................................................................................. III

TABLE OF CONTENTS ............................................................................................. IV

AUTHOR PROFILE .................................................................................................. VII

INTRODUCTION .................................................................................................... VIII

SETTING THE SCENE ................................................................................................ 1

    EXTREME IDEOLOGY AND THE SCIENTIFIC DEATH OF 'SOCIAL CONDITIONING' ........................ 1

SECTION 1 ................................................................................................................. 5

    WHY WE CAN'T 'TRANSCEND' OUR GENETICALLY-BASED SELVES ............................................ 5

SECTION 2 ............................................................................................................... 11

    CAUSATION IS UPWARDS: WHAT'S 'DOWNWARDS' IS JUST FEEDBACK .................................... 11

SECTION 3 ............................................................................................................... 16

    THE CORE BIOLOGICAL PRINCIPLE THAT DEALS WITH GENE COPYING MISTAKES ..................... 16

SECTION 4 ............................................................................................................... 19

    SEX IS PURGING FAULTY GENES BY A DIFFERENT MATING TYPE ............................................ 19

SECTION 5 ............................................................................................................... 22

    BOTH SEXES INVEST IN REPRODUCTION: FEMALES AFTER SEX, MALES BEFORE ....................... 22

SECTION 6 ............................................................................................................... 25

    THE KEY MALE 'GENETIC FILTER' MECHANISM: DOMINANCE HIERARCHY .............................. 25

SECTION 7 ............................................................................................................... 29

    HIERARCHY PROPER IS ONLY EVER AMONGST MALES ......................................................... 29

SECTION 8 ............................................................................................................... 35

    'POLICING' MALES THROUGH PREJUDICE ........................................................................... 35

SECTION 9 ............................................................................................................... 42

    A SEX-SPECIFIC STRESS MECHANISM UNDERPINS THE MALE DOMINANCE CONTEST ............... 42

| | |
|---|---|
| **SECTION 10** | **47** |
| HIERARCHY IS CENTRAL TO MALES FROM EARLIEST DEVELOPMENT | 47 |
| **SECTION 11** | **50** |
| BOYS / MEN GROUP ALL-INCLUSIVELY BEYOND THEIR HIERARCHY | 50 |
| **SECTION 12** | **53** |
| HOW WOMEN'S SOCIALITY ARISES FROM MEN'S: WOMEN 'MARRY OUT' | 53 |
| **SECTION 13** | **60** |
| THE 'QUEEN BEE' IS THE RAINY-DAY DEFAULT SOLE BREEDER | 60 |
| **SECTION 14** | **64** |
| PAIR-BONDING SERVES WOMEN, BUT NOT THROUGH MEN BEING PROVIDERS | 64 |
| **SECTION 15** | **67** |
| MEN'S 'MATE-GUARDING' IS NOT WHAT IT SEEMS | 67 |
| **SECTION 16** | **73** |
| WOMEN VALUE PAIR-BONDING MORE THAN MEN DO | 73 |
| **SECTION 17** | **76** |
| WOMEN ARE MUCH THE MORE VIOLENT TO THEIR PARTNERS | 76 |
| **SECTION 18** | **81** |
| IN 'TRADITIONAL' SOCIETIES, WOMEN VIE TO 'HONESTLY SIGNAL' FIDELITY | 81 |
| **SECTION 19** | **87** |
| THE FEMALE WITHIN THE MALE SOCIAL STRUCTURE | 87 |
| **SECTION 20** | **92** |
| WOMEN RISE BY BEING MORE CONSCIENTIOUS | 92 |
| **SECTION 21** | **96** |
| MEN REALLY ARE MORE COMPETITIVE; WOMEN BACK AWAY | 96 |
| **SECTION 22** | **101** |
| CROSS-SEX, IT'S SEXUAL DISPLAY, NOT CONTEST: MEN ACT, WOMEN FLAUNT | 101 |

**SECTION 23** ............................................................................................................................................. 105

The Myth Of 'Sexual Conflict': It's Actually A Within-Sex Phenomenon ................................... 105

**SECTION 24** ............................................................................................................................................. 110

Coda: The Symbosis Of The Sexes ....................................................................................... 110

**REFERENCES** ........................................................................................................................................... 111

**NOTES PAGES** ........................................................................................................................................ 134

**NOTES PAGES** ........................................................................................................................................ 135

**NOTES PAGES** ........................................................................................................................................ 136

**NOTES PAGES** ........................................................................................................................................ 137

**NOTES PAGES** ........................................................................................................................................ 138

# AUTHOR PROFILE

**Steve Moxon** researches the biological roots of human sociality, with a special interest in the sexes. The author of *The Woman Racket: The New Science Explaining How the Sexes Relate at Work, Play and in Society* (Imprint Academic), his subsequent cross-disciplinary review papers for scientific and other academic journals offer novel theories on topics regarding major sex differences; all emanating from a new understanding of the origin of the sexes.

He may be contacted at stevemoxon3@talktalk.net

# INTRODUCTION

This is a 'layman's guide' – for the interested rather than the merely general reader – to recent major scientific insights that together reveal a comprehensive, holistic understanding of the sexes: what actually distinguishes them and why. A much needed overview drawing together hitherto disparate topics outlining how several principles mutually relate; it's a simplified distillation and update of the several topics that are the subject of my review papers, which provide more detailed and precise accounts and further sources. [The papers can be found reproduced from their journal homes (mostly *New Male Studies*) at my website, stevemoxon.co.uk. All are included here in the references.]

Less, then, is this an update of my book, *The Woman Racket: The New Science Explaining How the Sexes Relate at Work, at Play and in Society*, which is a mix of science and anti-ideology polemic; though of course, the science within the book is updated here: it's the best part of a decade since publication and there have been startling developments in science in that time, not to mention improvements in my own understanding and conceptual formulation. In the book there was less in the way of development of scientific argument than here, with the particular topics being the focus and behind the selection of scientific findings more than the science gradually being unravelled.

No prior knowledge is assumed, so any other than common-knowledge scientific terms are either explained or replaced with less formal terms (where they are not too imprecise). Notably, instead of the formal, easily confused terms *intra-sexual / inter-sexual*, I use *within-sex / between-sex* (or *same-sex / cross-sex*). I do, however, use the word *sociality*, despite its unfamiliarity; because it's useful shorthand for *social system / dynamics*. One term I avoid using is *gender* (*sic*) – other than in 'scare' quotes. It's ideological rather than scientific, and implies the falsehood of 'social construction' instead of the reality of a biological base.

The text is looser, more expansive than would be the case if this were a journal paper. In keeping with this relative informality, instead of always fully indicating references, key research is introduced just through the full name of the lead author (or the two or three authors, if that's all there are). Other necessary supportive studies are tagged in the standard way of author surname + year, which, though more intrusive than numbering, makes it easier to look up a reference. Clutter within the text is kept to a minimum through not referencing non-contentious points which aren't primary.

Note that the first section of the book is an introduction before the start of the book proper, to outline the totalitarian current political scene that has effectively prevented discussion of the actual nature of the sexes instead to foist how an extremist anti-scientific view would have them be. The perspective here and throughout is from my home nation of England; so spellings likewise are English rather than American.

X

# SETTING THE SCENE

## EXTREME IDEOLOGY AND THE SCIENTIFIC DEATH OF 'SOCIAL CONDITIONING'

If not everyone, most people, today as ever, would say that men and women are dissimilar, and profoundly and essentially so. They would not accept that sex difference is a superficial product of some sort of 'cultural construct' as a fluid 'gender' (*sic*). In this, they would be accurate, as abundant scientific evidence attests and as will be outlined here. The current establishment, institutional over-riding of the hitherto perennial, ubiquitous view in favour of a wilful failure to understand the what/why of the distinction between the sexes – indeed, even that there *is* any distinction between the sexes more real than merely ostensible – is a hallmark of contemporary life unique to this time and this (Western, particularly Anglophone) culture. This perspective is not a scientific one but has come about through a now hegemonic extreme ideology: 'identity politics' (for a full, referenced account of its origin, development and nature, see my paper, *The Origin of 'Identity Politics' and 'Political Correctness'*).

The core of this is a novel view of men and women by way of an attempt, dating back to the late 1920s, to explain why, despite the predictions of Marxist theory, there had been no revolution in the West despite just such in relatively backward Russia. Western European Marxist intellectuals seized on Freud's then brand new notion of 'repression' (*sic*), notwithstanding that it was non-scientific – being unfalsifiable; that is, so ill-defined that any and every evidence, including that which is contradictory, can be interpreted as supportive. Along with the rest of 'psychoanalysis', 'repression' is now comprehensively discredited – see, for example, Richard Webster: *Why Freud Was Wrong* (Webster, 1995; 2005). 'Repression' was hijacked to be the putative mechanism by which 'the workers' had been prevented from becoming revolutionary; occasioned, it was held, by 'capitalism': but no explanation was offered as to how what is merely a system of trade could somehow have any, let alone sufficient agency to translate into a profound psychogenic permanently altered state.

With the majority of 'the workers' being male, and the male being nominally the 'head of the family', then men were considered to be the conduit rendering the whole family 'capitalist'. Females, by contrast, were considered simply the victims, notwithstanding that most women back then also were in the workplace, and impacted (or not) by 'capitalism' hardly neither more nor less than men. A help was the usual prejudice of regarding the male but not the female as agentic, together with females seen as those of middle-class imagination rather than of working-class reality. So it was that woman was portrayed as not the conduit of 'capitalism' but, through being a supposed victim, resisting it; at least potentially so. Here was a convenient basis of rescuing Marxist/Marxian philosophy and thereby salving the 'cognitive dissonance' experienced by Left thinkers. That 'the workers' were not in revolt now did not mean that the Marxist intelligentsia would be obliged to eat their hats. The ideological battle thenceforward shifted from 'the workers' versus 'the boss' to women against men. 'Class war' gave way to what eventually became characterised as 'the personal is political'.

With the rise of Hitler displacing the whole of the so-called Frankfurt School of Marxist intellectuals, then this 'neo-Marxism' went on to ferment not within European but American academia. During the period from the late 1930s through to the 1960s, this new political philosophy spread beyond Ivy League universities across higher education in the USA generally, inspiring student politics, and percolating down through the professions. It then really took off in the wake of its latching on to and co-opting, first, in 1968, the US 'civil rights' movement, and, in 1969, the 'Stonewall' campaign. Both of these were intuited to be partially realised 'revolutions', providing whole new 'classes' of people who could be portrayed as demonstrating resistance to 'capitalism'. With the attribution of victim status thereby widened from women to take in 'blacks' and 'gays' (and then, by no rational but naive 'sympathetic' extension, all ethnic minorities and lesbians – and, eventually, even 'trans-sexuals'), sometime after 1970 the transformation came to be dubbed 'identity politics'. The by now familiar triumvirate of 'female', 'BEM' and 'LGBT' badging to afford 'victim group' status was born.

A politics that came right down to 'pavement' level in the UK from the 1980s on (the 'anti-racism' and 'anti-sexism' hysterias of the time, in 'single issue' politics and radicalisation of local Labour Party organisation), it became sufficiently ubiquitous to take hold within institutions in the 1990s. By the 'noughties' it was fully the all-consuming, effectively unchallengeable extremist political stance often mis-labelled 'political correctness' that nowadays we see everywhere – and, indeed, in some ways we no longer see, in its being so ingrained that it's the background we take as read. The origins of 'identity politics' and an understanding of what it is have been lost in the mists of time. It is, after all, a protracted evolution across almost a century – or much earlier still, when you consider that notions of men *versus* women were presaged in the peculiar ideas of Engels. This precludes anyone having a sufficient overview in their life experience to grasp it. Only those who study it as history can get a handle on it. Not least through cultural amnesia, then, the core bizarre belief persists that any difference between men and women is an historical aberration caused by 'capitalism'. By this article of faith there is, supposedly, 'naturally' no distinction (other than in sex organs) between the sexes.

Previously, common understanding of what distinguished women from men may not always have been in line with any scientifically informed position; yet, wayward in some respects though it may well have been, usually there wasn't a serious contradiction. In the wake of 'identity politics' / 'PC' becoming mainstream, there emerged the politically driven claim that the only mode by which the sexes can be made in any way different in their nature is 'social conditioning' of what supposedly starts out for both sexes as an identical empty canvas (the supposed 'blank slate'). The utility of an extreme notion of 'social construction' of the brain, in the totalitarian mindset, is that there is then (it is imagined) the potential for all to be '*de*-constructed'. A self-fulfilling prophecy, it's an 'emperor's new clothes' scenario, where the assiduous imposition of 'speech codes' according to 'identity politics' imperative dissuades all but a brave or reckless few from daring to prick the illusory bubble.

As a putative mechanism with sufficient depth to rival biological explanation for anything like core behaviour and cognition, 'social conditioning' to provide the 'social construction' of the brain is scientifically dead, and has been for some time (Turkheimer, 2000; Turkheimer & Waldron, 2000; Plomin & Daniels, 1987). The brain conceptualised as an amorphous general-learning device that somehow organises itself in development out of nothing is a non-starter as an hypothesis, never mind as a fully-fledged theory. Any adherence to a notion that at root is 'social conditioning' is a naive position born of failing to appreciate that there is an infinite regress to biology. Even if a coherent case could be made that anything that is psychologically key is the product at root of 'social conditioning', the question always is begged: who/what is behind the 'social conditioning'? Any answer which also is in terms of 'social conditioning' in turn begs just the same question: who/what is behind the 'social conditioning' of the 'social conditioning'? This question/answer chain extends indefinitely down a bottomless well of non-explanation. Not only is there no relation between naive faith in 'social conditioning' and wider 'hard' science (that is, it has no 'external validity'), but it is inconsistent in its own terms (that is, it has no 'internal consistency' either). The 'social constructivist' view of the sexes is a self-contradiction of a sort that may hold in quantum mechanics and conjecturing a multiverse, but cuts no ice in psychology. The sexes are supposed identical, yet, at the very same time, one sex is held somehow to 'oppress' the other in some foundational way, through the nebulously envisaged structure or dynamic of 'patriarchy' [*sic*], which amounts to nothing less tautological than *maleness*. No sense can be made of putting these two groundless, non-scientific positions together. It would be impossible for males to somehow conspire putatively to 'oppress' in their 'patriarchy' [*sic*] – if, indeed, this was itself a coherent notion of some real phenomenon capable of being perpetrated – and for females not to do likewise if there were no such thing as sex difference. The two irreconcilable notions co-exist only in a perpetual flipping of one to the other; a mutual oscillation, that, like a set of clubs being juggled, is bound to come crashing down to earth at some point.

This extremism does not qualify as a 'theory', because (as with Freud, discussed above) it is set up as a data-proof fait accompli. Yet everything we know about the sexes is contra to either pole of the ideology. Data proofing is apparent only to adherents, as they shift discussion off any ground where it lands. The enormous pile of evidence against has made no impression on the permanent converts. No amount can ever lead to an abandonment, because the non-theory is 'unfalsifiable'. The basis of science, it hardly needs re-stating, is that any and every theory has to stand or fall on the evidence. In other words, theory has to have the potential to be shown to be false; otherwise it cannot be considered a theory, by definition. If anything and everything can be taken to be supporting evidence then there can have been nothing sufficiently defined worth the positing. It was so woolly as to be meaningless. Anyone can put up a conjecture – an hypothesis; but without evidence it doesn't even get to be a theory to then warrant further scrutiny. It can still become popular, though, if it's in line with a natural prejudice; and so it may be that popular attachment to the politically foisted false picture of the sexes might still survive beyond the time lag of the main thrust of scientific findings filtering down to wide appreciation. Currently, though, albeit discrete items of biology applying to men/women topics do get an airing in the media, and regularly, and increasingly; they are presented at best along the lines that 'the jury is out', and where an overall picture of the sexes as other than on the 'standard social science model' is never broached. The current continued denial and refusal to allow proper discussion is not sustainable, albeit quite when 'the dam will burst', as it were, is not possible to predict.

# Section 1

## Why We Can't 'Transcend' Our Genetically-Based Selves

Contrary to the now received wisdom, as I will outline at length, women & men are not a mix, with each individual occupying some place on a continuum of maleness-femaleness. Of course, in some ways of looking at the sexes, this is just how they seem: a melange of traits which so overlap in confusion that they coalesce into a 'bell curve' normal distribution. With respect to some traits or measures this may show, roughly, males tending towards one end and females the other; but more usually females predominate in the middle with males in overwhelming proportion at *both* ends. (As later I will explain, what underlies this recurrent pattern is itself sex-specific.) It is easy to cut across men/women in such a non-informative way to then falsely claim that there is no sex difference, or – the mantra you often hear – that there is more variation within than between the sexes. This has been claimed in respect of personality differences, but it's now apparent that this is an illusion through poor methodology.

Sex difference in personality has almost always been looked at in terms of the so-called 'big five' broad personality constructs. Marco Del Giudice realised that these are aggregations of traits, and as such they hide almost all sex differences, because most are at more specific trait level. If sex differences in two narrower traits go in the opposite direction, then they cancel each other out when they are viewed in broader terms, as from the perspective of the 'big five'. What is needed is a finer level of resolution: to 10 or 20 traits. This reveals a startling transformation. Personality turns out to be almost entirely distinct according to sex, with a mere 10% overlap between men and women. In other words, 90% of personality measures are sex-specific. That's a gap – an 'effect size' – as large as anything ever found in psychology (Del Giudice, Booth & Irwing, 2012). So yes, indeed: in non-interesting ways of looking at the sexes, there may be more variation within- than between-sex; yet in the most profound ways the sexes are chalk and cheese. Self-evidently, these major contrasts are what tell us about the basis of the sexes rather than the things that they share, which, as organisms needing to maintain themselves, necessarily they have in common. The whole point of science hardly is to report data 'noise': it's to find the ways through and around it to detect the clear underlying principles.

Men & women are not merely 'different'. Comprehensive scientific findings outlined here show that in important – the most important – respects they are dichotomous (dividing sharply in two), and necessarily so. We now know the root reason why sex *is* a binary condition, and why key mechanism is sex-specific. What is more, contrary to usual assumption, there is no prospect of any of this ever changing – on any time-scale. Not only cannot culture / environment / 'social construction' undermine or 'transcend' this, but instead can serve only to *reinforce and yet further entrench*. Let me explain. A simplistic but the still (for now) standard view is that genes and environment are of roughly similar importance in shaping how we develop into who we are, and that the social aspect of environment can override genetic predisposition to the extent effectively of nullifying it. This is wholly mistaken. What we perceive as the environment is anything but some massive multifarious impingement on the human organism which it struggles to deal with. The way in which we have evolved to sense and process the environment is as highly selected pertinent facets we anticipate and actively search out so as to effectively deal or interact with and utilise. Over evolutionary time we must have become extremely adept at this, to the extent of long being highly nuanced in our adaptations of both rigid behaviours and cognition to produce flexibility of response – bar rare natural cataclysms, for which no adaptation can prepare us in any case. That this is so and hardly could be otherwise is apparent from standard Information Theory. It's especially true of the overwhelmingly most crucial aspect of the environment: other people.

From how we have long evolved to interact with others, we construct culture; the neural basis of our facility to do which, has evolved only because it has the useful function of feeding back to fine-tune and reinforce the very underlying biology from whence it sprang. It could not have evolved otherwise. The same is true for all of the many animal species that also exhibit culture – just as with tool use, this supposed unique feature of mankind actually is shared with all sorts of even quite lowly other life-forms. Behaviour becomes more complex, nuanced and flexible, so that goals can be achieved in what may be a more roundabout but thereby more assured manner. Goals are more completely and more likely to be achieved. This is the very opposite of the unthinking position commonly held that we somehow move away from and even sever ties with biology to re-make ourselves anew along some novel trajectory. The reality is that anything new that seems significant actually is an elaboration of business-as-usual, leaving only the superficial, more incidental as being anything genuinely new; and this is going nowhere unless it turns out that it well serves underlying fundamentals, in which case it will be harnessed to still further bolster them. What underlies always calls the shots. Cultures across the world are remarkably similar, but we often don't appreciate this, in that we are strongly biased to see differences because much of culture is the creation of 'in-group' markers – badges to enable detection, confirmation and reinforcement of same-group membership (or, conversely, *non*-membership). The upshot is that the more complex is culture and any other superstructure built upon biology, then the *more* – not less – faithful we are to the expression of our genes. It might even be said that we are ever more the *slaves* to our genes just as we imagine that we are becoming free of them.

This is a fundamental insight understood by the English philosopher John Gray – not the *Venus & Mars* guy! – who points out, in his 2007 book, *Black Mass: Apocalyptic Religion and the Death of Utopia*, that it is *not* understood by Richard Dawkins; nor, even, by the premier philosopher of evolution, Daniel Dennett. Dawkins (1976) makes the false claim, which he neither evidences nor argues, that humans can somehow "rebel against the tyranny of the selfish replicators". Dawkins' error is obvious in the restriction of his claim to humans, when humans are not unique in any evolved dimension – to reiterate: not in tool use, nor culture … nor, even, 'consciousness' (as all formerly were falsely claimed) – but instead are contiguous with other, especially primate, species. The mistake is through moving beyond the eminent evolutionist's expertise in science into philosophy. [Dawkins repeatedly in the media makes another error along these lines in claiming that religion can be argued away with scientific evidence, showing a lack of understanding that religiosity stems not from any attempt to explain the world, but instead functions to help to cope with the self-evident ultimate unanswerability in scientific terms of the really big questions.] Dennett, on the other hand, is a philosopher by trade, yet likewise betrayed a similar mistaken notion in his book-length exposition that "freedom evolves" (Dennett, 2003) without realising that what actually he is outlining as evolving is flexibility in how our biology via our genes is expressed; not any freedom *from* it. In citing the evolutionary biologist Edward O Wilson's famous metaphor of culture being in effect held "on a leash" from biology, attached to but allowing leeway to culture (Wilson, 1978), Dennett selects a metaphor extended beyond its breaking point. Unlike the pet dog on its master's lead, culture is derived from and part and parcel of its biological master. Whereas the pet dog is freer to act more naturally – to be less like, or to be less obedient to its owner – the further it is from being at its master's heel, the apparent freedom of culture is at the behest of its biological parent; as a controlled experiment to see if the offspring mechanism can helpfully augment parental expression so as to render the parent mechanism still truer to itself, as it were.

Professor of evolutionary psychology, Steven Pinker (1997), joined in this fray – by way of what seemed to be a pitch to get social scientists to board the evolutionary express instead of them trying to derail it – in his claim that he had personally defeated the evolutionary imperative to reproduce in being intentionally childless (that is, so far as he knew). "If my genes don't like it, they can go jump in the lake", is his oft-quoted rather rash assertion in this regard – from his book, *How the Mind Works*. In a sense, indeed he could be said to have thwarted natural imperative, but in the more important ways the claim is false. The eminent professor seems for once to forget what he must well know: that our motivation is not to reproduce per se, but is indirect in a desire for sex. [Well, this is true of men: most women do appear to become 'broody'; though, oddly, this is a still very thinly researched topic.] We are biological machines built on a 'need-to-know' principle: sex automatically leads to reproduction but for the use of the technology of contraception, re which the evolutionary process hardly has had time to take into account – however, evolved adaptation is behind why it is that women who ('consciously' or not) wish to conceive, do so readily by implicitly motivated 'bodging' of the contraception (see Eisenman, 2003). More to the point, high-fertility women potentially would be very willing to pair-bond or have uncommitted ('extra-pair') sex with a male of such high status as is a pre-eminent professor; his high status having been acquired through male competitiveness driven by genes for the very function of attracting the opposite sex (as is fully explained here in due course). Our pre-eminent evolutionary psychologist has not spilled the beans about his sex life, and nor should he feel obliged to do so; but it's highly unlikely that a man in his station would entirely resist myriad temptation. Even if he had been Jesus-like to the point of not even a single lapse, then the superhuman effort he would have needed would rather give the lie to his claim. A contrarian renegade merely reveals quite how perverse you have to be to avoid behaving according to genetic predisposition or prescription. The point is that the vast majority of others who get themselves into this sort of high-ranking position would have no trouble and every enthusiasm in succumbing to sexual temptation.

For an adaptive response to continue to work well, it does not require universal conformity. As little as a significant statistical bias would suffice. Even as regards key motivations, other components of our motivational set are bound to enter the fray to cloud what seems to be going on, producing as much or more 'noise' than effect; albeit that in this case there is little other than the main effect, given that almost all males feel highly driven to partake of sex when it is in the offing. It might more accurately be said, then, that the professor's genes told *him* to go jump in the lake! Any protest that the charge was invalid would hold water about as well as a retort: "but I was wearing a wet suit".

Pinker, Dennett and Dawkins, being perhaps the three most eminent evolutionary thinkers … these, out of all people, should have realised and ought to be labouring the point that we could never 'transcend', as it were, our genetically driven mindsets. It seems, as so often with those too close to the epicentre of the vortex of thought in their discipline – and particularly if also they feel obliged to go with the flow, nay tidal wave of current political imperative – that they could not see the wood for the trees, despite their attempts at forensic dissection. For the perception to flip from 'tree' to 'wood' requires the fresh perspective of outsiders.

## Section 2

# Causation is Upwards: What's 'Downwards' is Just Feedback

Causation is upwards, with its subjection to a constellation of feedback loops giving the appearance that causation is (or is also) downwards. This is how it can be imagined that society or the 'environment' is the key cause rather than biology. There is, of course, a political intrusion here: of a serious misunderstanding and misrepresentation of determinism as if somehow eliminated from consideration are chance, complexity and conflicting causes. It unravels as soon as you consider the contrasting reaction to the expressions 'genetic determinism' and 'environmental determinism'. If the supposed problem was positing *determinism* per se, then objection would be the same to either. The big fuss is over positing any genetic/biological causation at all, because this challenges the political notion of no limits to the malleability of human psychology, which would be necessary to impose a political system denying the reality of human nature in the round in favour of a focus on only one aspect of it, in line with Marxian collectivist philosophy.

The expression 'downward causation' was coined and developed in the 1960s and 1970s to be elaborated into both 'strong' and 'weak' forms in the 1990s, but it has fallen out of favour. A recent neat demolition is by Sean Carroll (2011), who attributes the notion to the egocentricity of human psychology. Some try to argue it by positing the intervention of stages of 'emergence', whereby a qualitatively different new level becomes established in that it is, supposedly, more than the sum of its parts. An illusion, again: the mistake here is to envisage a discrete entity and in this focus fail to appreciate massive interconnectedness. The philosopher Mark Bedau (Bedau & Humphreys, 2008) sees all notions of 'emergence' as problematising by philosophers. In other words, it's an invention so as to provide pontification around which philosophers can bid for glory: status. Hence extraordinarily convoluted discussions, such as *The Disturbing Matter of Downward Causation: A Study of the Exclusion Argument and its Causal Explanatory Presuppositions*; an inconclusive work by Øistein Schmidt Galaaen (2006), which he sets in a field within philosophy he sees as 'work in progress'. It seems more like a 'treasure at the end of the rainbow' to keep philosophers in indefinite employ.

Similarly, some theorists have conceptualised culture as a newly emerged entity ('niche') which then exerts some novel form of evolutionary selective pressure; but this is merely an over-fancy, indeed misleading way of labelling what is nothing more than usual feedback looping inherent in already well-outlined mechanism. It's a normal part of natural selection (Dickins & Dickins, 2008). Arguing for a profundity to 'niche construction' has been dismissed as falling foul of basic Information Theory and revisiting Dawkins' (1989) conceptualisation of the 'extended phenotype' – the effect genes have, through the organism for which they code, on the organism's own environment, setting up reflexive feedback looping, such that genes self-reinforce and fine-tune through their own effects – but only in merely re-stating it (European Science Foundation, 2008; Dawkins, 2004). 'Niche Construction', if it could be afforded the status of a theory, is one in need of a reason to exist, other than the self-aggrandisement of its proponents. Not merely does this contravene the paramount principle in science of parsimony, but obfuscates through pointless elaboration.

The ultimate expression of a supposed 'downward causation' is the founding statement of sociology by its father, Emile Durkheim, in his claim that there are irreducible 'social facts'. On the very contrary, all social phenomena – even the most seemingly ultra collective – Dawn Kitchen & Craig Packer (1999) have shown to be explicable from the level of the individual. To do so is not 'greedy reductionism', as Dennett (1996) might too warily warn; though, of course, appealing to 'first principles' without acknowledging any intermediate level of analysis might well be guilty of the charge.

It's simply that in any account we must work 'bottom-up', not 'top-down'. Working 'top-down' is to encompass all of the forms of instrumental conceits and self-deceits to which biology has given rise through evolution in our psychology: in the very lens through which we are looking in order to come up with explanation. The result is a tautology, where ideology is recycled into the very distortion of a supposed science that gave rise to the ideology in the first place. So much sociology and social psychology is a closed-off field of self-validating ideology-bound constructs. Ideology (religiosity and aspects of the content) is itself a product of biology requiring explanation in biological terms. Trying to explain ideology in terms of itself is non-explanation to the point where it's just a refusal to allow investigation.

We fail to grasp that causation is 'bottom-up' through our astonishingly inflated estimation of what we can get our minds round. Yes, we can work up erudite argument (as, I would hope, I'm doing here) but it does not at all follow that we are fully or even vaguely knowledgeable of our motivational wellsprings – even as, necessarily, we are very much in touch with them through how they translate into our emotions – and certainly not that we can figure them out simply by self-reflection. Such conceit is contradicted by all of the research into consciousness. Not some but all cognition occurs without our being in any way aware of it. We are aware only afterwards, and even then only of an infinitesimally small fraction. Our seeming obvious sense that we make decisions in the real time of our conscious consideration is wholly illusory. For all that philosophers endlessly stretch arcane argument, everything known about the brain reveals that there is no 'top-down' seat of command. Conscious awareness seems to be nothing more than an epiphenomenon of the integration of our neural processing; an afterglow of cognition. There is no control centre somewhere in the frontal cortex as we assume. Instead, the brain is a highly integrated set of feedback loops, just as would be expected from the new perspective of systems-biology. [This is outlined in the 2008 book by Denis Noble, *The Music of Life*, but the strength of the tendency to revert to form shows through even here. For all of Noble's emphasis on connectivity over locus, nevertheless he allows default habits of thinking to mistake feedback looping for 'downward causation'.] The human brain can be envisaged as something like an onion. It embodies its evolutionary history in a succession of distinct layers, each of which evolved successively to take inputs from all of the layers below to integrate them and feed the new assimilation back down, and so on in endless looping. If we had to identify some part of the brain as a source of direction, then we'd have to cite the brain-stem and associated primitive (evolutionarily very ancient) portions of what is dubbed the 'old brain', beneath the cortex and the rest of the cerebrum, named the limbic system. These are loci of motivations and how they become manifest as emotions. And just as all brain activity arises from the very base and oldest part of the central nervous system, so this, in turn, springs from core biology and its genetic encoding.

It might well be objected that the circularity within the brain cannot but produce a corresponding circularity of explanation, never mind being able to distinguish between 'bottom-up' and 'top-down' as to which is efficacious. But this is to ignore how, in effect, we can step outside the routine workings of the brain to capture and test insight, and then check it collectively, to catch hold of a step-up in understanding before it falls back: ratcheting up checkable knowledge instead of it always reverting to base or forever chasing its tail. Science. Whereas (as I have argued) we can never transcend ourselves, as it were, this is in a meta sense, personally, regarding our individual and social behaviour. We regularly push things some way before our evolved imperatives return to subvert and co-opt what we're doing. But science is an extra-individual, and indeed, in important senses, not an extra-collective – in any normal social sense – way that we can go beyond this. It's almost super-human, it might be said, in its disengagement from human psychological and sociological usual functioning. It's a set-up explicitly to get round the limitations of usual ways of both thinking and interacting.

There is no theoretical, philosophical obstacle to painstakingly amassing an internally consistent body of knowledge that, through persistent testing against data from the environment, is a reliable reflection of an actual reality rather than one subsumed under the reproductive imperatives of how the brain has evolved to function. In other words, it also has an external validity. It is true that in the end this must come up against the limitations that our reproduction-geared minds can handle – hence religiosity to cope with unfathomable ultimate questions, like 'what drives evolution?' Or 'how can there be nothing beyond the edge of the universe?' Yet a workable reconstruction of 'reality' sufficient to enhance our lives with technology and, even, to go some way towards properly understanding ourselves so that we can, for example, treat schizophrenia … such demonstrably have been achieved. Yes, it's hard to do and has limitations; and given that ultimately it breaks down, then it might be considered that I'm resurrecting the Dawkins/Pinker/Dennett axis I've criticised. Certainly, scientists in their very activity are, from the perspective of their personal and group behaviour, fulfilling biological imperative re seeking and gaining status; but this does not mean that the *content* of their activity is also governed by the same co-option.

As a parallel: a railway modeller is exercising and developing his skills, and seems to be seeking to control his environment; feeling a need to do this that stems ultimately from a motivation to bid for status. His loft-filling layout is, however, simply a concerted effort to construct a working facsimile of reality in which he can lose himself. Probably, it's an evocation of a lost world from his youth, less any negative facets. It's one within which there is no embodiment of the modeller's intrinsic motivation to acquire some sort of pre-eminence over others. It may well be an escape from such expectations, or a fantasy version of how to live life according to these imperatives – as with the train-spotter, who is engaging in competitive hierarchical behaviour, even if he's lost the plot in his choice of arena, given that the underlying name of the game is attracting females! Either way, this is meta in a very distant sense from the content. And so it is for Pinker (1997) vis-a-vis his work per se, not least his aforementioned book, *How The Mind Works*; despite the way that biological imperative is so key to Pinker's striving and achieving professorship. Even if there were some force to the charge of resurrecting the very Dawkins/Pinker/Dennett axis I criticised, in science we can escape it, at least to a degree. And the point is that to the extent we can succeed, to do so we have to get down to 'first principles' and then build back up, to check it's possible to systematically construct a model corresponding to gross observable phenomena. If we are even to try to escape thinking in ways hopelessly compromised by the very brain processes we seek to understand, the only way of working is 'bottom-up'.

# Section 3

## The Core Biological Principle That Deals with Gene Copying Mistakes

With ultimately all stemming from biology, so that gene-'environment' interaction is a hall-of-mirrors extension of genetic influence; the next question is: what, ultimately, is the core principle in biology driving everything? As everyone well knows, for all of the 'plumbing', as it were – all the overt mechanism that allows the body to do what it has to do to survive – there is a genetic blueprint. There has to be a hierarchically organised array of genes that repeatedly have to be copied into new cells to enable growth by the original single fertilised egg multiplying and differentiating, eventually to produce a full-size body, and after that to replace cells that become worn-out. Unfortunately, at each and every instance of gene replication there is a vast number of possibilities for some sort of error, and these are cumulative. Despite highly effective repair mechanisms (some of which are only now being discovered), the occasional error is not caught, and given the enormous number of genes and the huge number of times they are copied, then each individual will have hundreds or thousands of instances of previously fully functioning genes that, in some tissues, to varying degrees, become duff. There may be an accidental small change in one of the nitrogenous 'bases' of DNA responsible for coding – a mutation – or a change to how genes are inter-related in their hierarchy of regulation; or just a novel juxtaposition of genes that counteract each other in some way. Any of these sorts of changes are very much more likely to cause some dysfunction than to be beneficial. Eventually, the load of deleterious genetic change renders the individual biologically non-viable. In order words, you die; or you live but you're infertile; or you're physiologically or behaviourally impaired such that you haven't got the wherewithal to reproduce, or nobody would want to join with you in reproducing. In the end, we all get this way in the process we call ageing. In any of these cases, the whole individual organism then needs to be replaced. This is why reproduction is central to biology. We intuit that survival is king, with reproduction some bonus add-on; but reproduction is not instrumental to survival: it's the other way round. Survival per se is of no importance. It's merely the time the reproductive entity takes to reproduce, after which the organism is done. Whether or not it limps on is an irrelevance. There can be no selection pressure for longevity beyond when reproduction ceases. It might seem otherwise, but not when you consider that for women this is when reproduction is fully completed, after caring for offspring until viability as young adults. For men, it's when their potential to inseminate ends, which, even ancestrally, was well into their 50s; which facilitated a disproportionately high fecundity of high-status males down the ages (as revealed by DNA analysis). The enormous reproductive skew amongst men is what drove the evolution of not just their own greater longevity but that of humans generically (human longevity has been supposed to be the result of childcare provided by grandmothers). There can be no survival with any point to it, and no evolution, even to the very first base of the most primitive life-form possible, without reproduction. Necessarily, genes have to be primarily concerned with preventing themselves from being degraded. This is what all life is about; in essence, the staving off of otherwise inevitable entropy – disorder – by a seemingly miraculous self-sustaining assemblage.

This is the key problem hardly just for the individual. Extinction would be inevitable without some mechanism to solve it. Such foundational mechanism would be primordial to all but the absolute beginning of the evolution of life; pretty well *the* oldest evolutionary product – phylogenetically the most ancient – which thereafter would have to have been consistently very highly conserved through all evolutionary time. To couch in 'levels of selection' terms: whereas throughout evolution selection is usually considered to be at the 'individual' level, at key points of major transition selection is at higher, ultimately not merely 'group' but 'species' level (Okasha, 2008; Maynard, Smith & Szathmary, 1995). I say this to dispel stale rhetorical charges of effectively invoking 'group selection' (*sic*), which, even if such charges were here applicable, recent theoretical research reveals to be misguided. I'm not talking about the reformulation of 'group selection' (Novak, Tarnita & Wilson, 2010) to try to get round the clear objection to its 'naive' version, which Dawkins famously and rightly argued. Now-standard 'population genetics' models (Keller, 1999) and alternatives involving population structure (Powers, Penn & Watson,

2011; Lion, Jansen & Day, 2011) or 'lineage selection'(Nunney, 1999) are all mathematically equivalent, and, therefore, empirically interchangeable; that is, both with each other and with a 'levels of selection' analysis – as I explain at several junctures in my published papers. Really, all models straddle the conceptual divide between selection acting on the individual and 'population genetics', and amount to an appreciation of 'inclusive fitness': that selection acts in effect at between the 'individual' and 'group' levels, through the genetic similarity of individuals within the local population in their being (usually) distant if not close relatives. My point here is that this is not controversial within science. It may be controversial to those who have not followed developments since argument when Dawkins' book, *The Selfish Gene*, was still current as a significant corrective to wayward thinking about evolution.

In this context, individuals are expendable, as are whole 'groups' – lineages. Simple continued replication would suffice even if say 99% or 99.9% of individuals not possessing a near-optimal genome can be allowed simply to go to the wall. This is how simple organisms such as those of bacterial species survive and rapidly evolve. Each individual is microscopic, requiring next to zero development, and not required to be viable for any longer than a flash in time; so the investment per individual is insignificant. Even in respect of whole lineages, investment is so minimal as barely to register. The vast majority of entire lineages of bacteria rapidly become evolutionary dead-ends. There is, however, an alternative way to deal with accumulated gene replication error. This is to render each individual much more robust, so that they can survive to be compared one with the other – or battle each other – and only then do those individuals possessing a sub-optimal genomic complement go to the wall. This means evolving into a far more complex organism. The trouble with this strategy is that it entails much more investment in each individual, making them less expendable. This calls for some new safe-guarding mechanism to prevent the now substantial investment being too easily lost. Here is where sex enters the fray. [Note that this is how sex came to be utilised after sex cells became differentiated into a small and a large (by this definition the female) mating type. How sex initially *arose* is a different matter, which I briefly discuss much later when I finally come on to the supposed phenomenon of 'sexual conflict'.]

# SECTION 4

## SEX IS PURGING FAULTY GENES BY A DIFFERENT MATING TYPE

To deal with the accumulation of gene replication error, instead of straight copying (cloning) of genes, what is thought to be key to sex – and clearly is a very important part of sex – is the aspect of sex with which everyone is familiar. It's that a random half of the genome of each of two individuals end up fused together, following genes having been separated and mixed up. 'Recombination' certainly does radically dislocate any concentrations of harmful mutations or gene clusters there may be, so that in the (very) short term it would solve the problem of gene replication error; but beyond the short-term this proves illusory. In the absence of recombination, 'dodgy' genes would tend by chance in a good few cases to coalesce, rendering some individuals too dysfunctional to reproduce. Just by the usual workings of probability, then, quite a decent slice of 'bad' genes would be lost from the local gene pool – 'purged' is the term used in biology. Yet this is prevented in sex by the recombination process having the effect of dislocating such coalescence to fairly evenly distribute and hence dilute deleterious genetic material across most or all individuals, which then makes it more difficult in the end to identify and eliminate 'bad genes' from the gene pool, thereby undermining the very process which supposedly evolved to deal with the accumulation of gene replication error. Recombination on its own, then, actually proves counter-productive (Paland & Lynch, 2006).

What actually is key to the success of sex is less recombination than there being two separate mating types. If all there were to sex was recombination, then there would be no reason why all individuals couldn't be hermaphrodites (each and every individual having both male and female sex organs). In some primitive species, where there is alternation between mainly asexual and occasional sexual reproduction, individuals may be hermaphrodites. By mating '69' style, as it were – individual A's penis inserting into individual B's vagina, and individual A's vagina being inserted by individual B's penis – not only can both parties conceive internally to gestate and give birth to offspring, but they produce offspring which are all genuinely genetically recombined. For almost all sexually reproducing species, however, the different sex organs never co-occur in the same individual. Invariably, half of individuals have a penis and only a penis, whereas the other 50% have a vagina and only a vagina. This is a profound change from the hermaphrodite condition, because it means that only half of the number of individuals are produced than would be the case with either asexual or sexual hermaphroditic reproduction. There has to be an equally profound reason for this. Why would it have evolved that half the population forgo actual reproduction itself, instead merely to supply a small sex cell to fuse with a much larger one? If both sexes nurtured eggs (the sex cells that are much larger through being loaded with nutrients) and gave birth, then reproduction would be twice as efficient.

Well, this ... what has been thought to be the weakness of sex, actually is its strength. In marking out half of individuals to focus on reproduction – conceiving the fertilised egg, gestating it, giving birth and nurturing offspring to adulthood – they can then be freed from the struggle to deal with accumulated gene replication error, if this were to become the duty of the other 50% of individuals. This is the task assigned to males. It's the foundational reason why there *are* males. Note that (pair-bonding aside) although only a proportion, even just a small proportion of males are required to impregnate all females; nevertheless males always constitute half the population or nearly so. Females never increase in proportion to much more than 50%. A half-and-half split turns out to be an evolutionarily stable equilibrium to which any skew in relative proportion returns; though the reason for this is incidental to and anyway beyond the scope of the present account. A window on how crucial is the male is the discovery in 2014 by Laurent Boulanger and her team, that, contrary to what has long been assumed, the default sex is *not* the female. Everyone, male and female both, would develop into males in the absence of genetic intervention. XY individuals automatically become male, and likewise would those with XX sex chromosomes, unless FOXL2 and several other genes are expressed.

Sex had long been thought to have evolved so as to produce variation: a wider range of genetic recombinations for selection to act upon, thereby to help prevent local or even species extinction at times of unusual ecological stress – prolonged droughts, volcanic winters, etc – and/or so as to keep up with or at least not to fall too far behind in a 'red queen' battle with injurious microbes and parasites in their fast-evolving mechanisms to outwit all efforts by the host to expel them. This, though, was a view of the sexual process that focused on the recombination of genes in sex whilst ignoring the separation of the two contrasting mating types. Variation is better conceptualised as the other, positive side of the coin to dealing with the accumulation of gene replication error. It's complementary to, though really subsumed by this, the more primary function. The notion of a crucial importance to variation stems from the above-cited error of envisaging 'environment' as unexpected and uncontrollable factors impinging on the unprepared organism, when in fact the vast bulk of the pertinent facets of 'environment' are others of your own species, which in common with other salient facets of the environment the entire evolutionary history has fully prepared you to anticipate, seek out, process, and fruitfully interact with. What counts is being able effectively to deal with other individuals – as either competitors or potential sexual partners, according to whether they are of the opposite or the same sex. It's not variation but getting rid of accumulated gene replication error that protects against rare ecological disaster from causing local or species extinction. It's highly unlikely that a recent mutation or genetic recombination will confer some protection from cataclysmic events sufficient to mean that a very few could have changed in just the right way so as to weather the storm. It's much more likely that with the population maintained at an optimum or near maximum fitness, a few, stronger or particularly well-adjusted individuals will manage by the skin of their teeth to hang on.

Evolution appears to be a trajectory of increasing reproductive efficiency to progressively minimise wastage of investment – not that this is teleological (moving towards some final outcome as if it were being pulled by and towards it, rather than a playing out to go wherever it will from initial causes). Of course, this is not created in the course of evolution so much as inherent in the very process that *is* evolution, because without it evolution could not occur. It could never have got started. The more refined is both the male-male contest to establish the more reproductively fit males and the choosing of these males by females, then the higher becomes the genetic quality and (if not in the shorter then in the longer term) the number of offspring, which significantly improves the viability of the local reproductive population if and when there appears an unusual serious environmental stress that might threaten local extinction.

## SECTION 5

## BOTH SEXES INVEST IN REPRODUCTION: FEMALES AFTER SEX, MALES BEFORE

Hitherto, the difference between the sexes has been thought to be that the female is the investing sex. Certainly, the female invests in offspring, in the aftermath of sex. Not only is the female unique in gestating, giving birth, lactating, and providing prolonged very close care of offspring; but, even in the human case, females are twice as likely to have at least one offspring. DNA analysis in 2004 by Jason Wilder, Zahra Mobasher & Michael Hammer reveals that ancestrally whereas the great majority (80%) of women reproduced, only a minority (40%) of men did so. Across evolutionary time, men on average had just half the chance of reproducing compared to women. That investment after sex is always more so for females than for males is known as Bateman's Principle (after a 1948 paper by the geneticist Angus Bateman). This principle still holds, notwithstanding instances of ostensible 'sex reversal' where the *male* cares for the young. This is often the case with ground-nesting birds (and seahorses), for the reason that the female has to invest far more than is usual for birds in egg production in anticipation of heavy predation of the far more vulnerable eggs. What has been missing is any understanding of the very different but no less if not far more important form of investment made by the male, which is not after but *before* sex.

The process to deal with the core problem in all biological systems in effect is quarantined on the male side of the lineage. In contrast to females, the job of the males is for their genes to be radically exposed to natural selection, so that those males displaying, relatively, some form of deficiency or less than prowess, through possession of a sub-optimal, below-average, or a simply not pre-eminent genome, are identified for weeding out, to take with them their deleterious genetic material, which thereby is eliminated from the local gene pool. This overall process has been dubbed the '(male) genetic filter', by the pioneering biologist and computer engineer Wirt Atmar (1991), in his key paper 'On the Role of Males'. Apparently unaware of Atmar's work, in 2005, Mary Jane West-Eberhard termed it the 'mutational cleanser' – though this last is inaccurate in that mutation is only a part of the deleterious genetic change that may occur in genetic recombination; so I prefer to use Atmar's term.

That this process indeed occurs is shown by selection overall acting much more on males than on females. This was long regarded as being obvious and not an empirical question. There is plenty of indirect evidence (Whitlock & Agrawal, 2009), and previously it had been modelled (Siller, 2001; Agrawal, 2001; West-Eberhard, 2005), but methodological issues had to be overcome in order actually to test it. Confirmation in actual data has been repeated, independently by a succession of researchers (Singh & Artieri, 2010; Mallet et al, 2011; McGuigan. Petfield & Blows, 2011; Campos, Charlesworth & Haddrill, 2012; Wright & Mank, 2013; Harrison et al, 2015). A team led by Alyson Lumley (2015) conclude explicitly that "sexual selection protects against extinction". The extra purging of deleterious genetic material from the gene pool through the male half of the lineage is sufficient to more than compensate for sexual reproduction requiring two parents to make each offspring rather than just the one needed in asexual reproduction (the famous 'twofold cost of sex' I alluded to). New modelling in 2015 by Denis Rose and Sarah Otto reveals that sex cannot persist at all unless there is more selection on males than on females. It would quickly die out.

So how is it that there is much more selection, both natural and sexual, acting on males? Well, first, it is clear, from the work last year by James Crowley and a large team, that there is much more male than female genetic material for selection to act upon; that is, everyone inherits much more male genetic material *that actually is expressed*. This is through so-called 'imprinting' (an allele is 'tagged' as being from the male parent and when it's transcribed in offspring the tag renders it dominant to other alleles) and another process not understood creating a skew in favour of male-derived alleles. One of Crowley's team, Pardo-Manuel de Villena, said: "We now know that mammals express more genetic variance from the father. So imagine that a certain kind of mutation is bad. If inherited from the mother, the gene wouldn't be expressed as much as it would be if it were inherited from the father" (Crowley et al, 2015).

So there is bound to be much more selection of male-derived genetic material, but this is inherited by females as well as males. There must also be something about the selection process itself that strongly biases towards sifting the male-derived genetic material *within males*. How is it done? Well, it's not just through death, of course; albeit that males certainly die off – notably when young – far more than do females. But this is a symptom; a blatant product of sex-differential selection. The male weeding-out part of the process can be achieved in a number of ways; most obviously, female mate-selection criteria can be set to choose only better-quality males. Very importantly, males can help females make their choices by fiercely contesting amongst themselves; not least in physical fighting. This extreme stress exposes those males with less genetic fitness – even if in absolute terms they are really quite fit indeed; what matters is relative fitness. The process drives relentless fitness improvement, even if there seems only a limited scope. In consequence, the 'dodgy' genes that tend to accumulate are perennially mostly purged. In male physical contest, though some males may be killed or injured, and in that blunt way removed from the reproductive stakes; more subtly, fighting and the various other modes of male-male contest for prestige can sort out the men from the boys, as it were.

In this way, some, many or even most males eventually shy away and leave the coast clear for the winning males either to take the initiative with and/or to appeal to females who then may actively choose them. Well, maybe eventually some or most males may give up, but with the stakes so high, then few males are likely to give up even with odds heavily stacked against them. Sheer belligerence may win through a shortfall in physical strength. It would seem, then, that no-holds-barred conflict would result in even the winners sustaining heavy costs, compromising their ability to reproduce just when they have won the right to do so. And with so much ongoing contest, it would be hard for females to suss just who were the winners as opposed to losers unless they were keen and persistent observers. It might instead be better, then, for male-male contest to be more ordered: for it to be ritualised such that a fairly reliable measure of relative possession of 'good genes' is recorded in some enduring way so as to obviate further contest.

# Section 6

## The Key Male 'Genetic Filter' Mechanism: Dominance Hierarchy

Enter dominance hierarchy. Well, at least this (rendering further contest unnecessary) is how it has been assumed that dominance hierarchy confers a benefit. Another assumption is that it works as regards vying for any kind of resources, with 'resources' taken to be anything and everything material, running to include the female body, as if access to sex were just another resource issue. That this is not the case is clear if you try to work out the ranking within an animal group from observing contest in different competition scenarios; for example, over food, compared to nesting sites, or mates. Typically, you end up with a different rank order for each scenario (Lanctot & Best, 2000). The usual understanding of dominance hierarchy is only provisional, being informed more than anything by the considerable practical difficulties in how data is collected: how to assess rank order from interactions. Often 'sub-dominance' is assumed despite there being nothing signalled, likely confusing it with deference. There is a real problem of 'garbage in' / 'garbage out' obfuscation (Fedigan, 1992). For further outline, see my paper on dominance hierarchy (Moxon, 2009).

The formation of a hierarchy is the local allocation of rank according to either physical prowess and/or belligerent attitude – dominance as ordinarily understood – and/or prestige ('prestige dominance'); all of which being good overall measures of genetic quality. An individual male can belong to a number of different dominance or prestige hierarchies; these varying greatly in scale, with some nested inside much wider status pyramids. To be able to participate in any one of these, all individuals constituting the ranking have to be equipped with the evolved requisite brain circuitry to process so-called 'winner' and/or 'loser' effects (Dugatkin & Earley, 2004). It's not hierarchy itself that evolved, of course: that's simply an epiphenomenon – of the interaction of individuals in possession of the necessary neural kit. 'Winner' and/or 'loser' effects are algorithms (sequential sets of decision rules) encoded in neuronal connections that separately bias each individual to be either more or less predisposed to seek or accept future contest according to their own past success or failure; this being re-set after each contest. In this way, rank predicts the outcome of contests, such that ranking is fully 'transitive' – by this is meant that if an individual, A, is dominant to another individual, B, and B is dominant to yet another individual, C; then it can be correctly inferred that A is also dominant to C. A big benefit of this is that there is then no need for each and every individual to contest each and every other individual in the group in a total set of all possible permutations of contest. A partial permutation suffices. We know that this is how it all works from Charlotte Hemelrijk's (2000) 'Domworld' computer modelling of autonomous cyber agents able to process 'winner' and/or 'loser' effects: this indeed does produce a fully transitive – 'linear' – hierarchy.

This mechanism clearly would serve to avoid unnecessarily persistent male-male contest, but is this all it does? Is this even its main function? Actually, is this its function *at all*? To reiterate: with the stakes so high, then few males are likely to give up 'chasing skirt' even with odds heavily stacked against them. It would pay to up sheer belligerence despite being relatively short, or not thick-set, or lacking in muscle power; however you were disadvantaged in the mating game. That the males who end up on-top having come through such a testy, protracted battle would thereby more effectively show their mettle, and that they can successfully engage in courtship and sex notwithstanding the damage they may well have sustained ….. serves all the more to indicate their complement of 'good genes'. This is known in biology as 'honest signalling'. Females will be wise to males trying to make out that they are something they are not, so anything which 'keeps them honest' will better oil the mating stakes.

What in fact is happening here, is that male-on-male battling is self-dampening. Losing one or two contests, so that you are pushed down the rankings, feels stressful. This psychological and physiological condition is caused by low rank being registered in the secretion of higher levels of the main stress hormone, cortisol. Crucially, cortisol is 'antagonistic' to testosterone; that is, cortisol feeds back to inhibit testosterone production. This reduces fertility, both physiologically – sperm production, etc – and behaviourally – the propensity to pursue females; and, indeed, to contest with other males to try to gain in rank (which in turn would reverse the fall in testosterone levels). In this way, rank translates into the equivalent, appropriate likelihood (or not) of reproducing. Whereas lower ranked males are automatically hindered, so that commensurately they reproduce little or not at all; higher ranked males would be left free to reproduce. Actually, it works even better than this, in that for higher-ranked males their propensity to reproduce is not merely unhindered but actually is boosted through their being rendered unaffected by cortisol – excessive levels, that is; moderate levels of cortisol are required to facilitate assertion. As Robert Sapolsky's team (listed as Abbott, 2003) briefly review, for high-status males only, a protein is produced preventing cortisol above a moderate level from binding with its receptor. This means that high levels of cortisol circulating in the bloodstream won't result in a deleterious experience of stress, but instead the impact will be a beneficial one. The biochemistry of this has been traced in some primates (which almost certainly will be the same as in humans), and other mechanisms further refining the impact of cortisol are likely to be revealed given that even in relatively lowly classes of species (fish) no less than four different types of cortisol receptor have been discovered (Greenwood et al, 2003).

We know this mechanism to block the effects of high levels of cortisol in high-status males applies to human males from the enormous 'Whitehall' studies on stress and civil servants famously conducted by the epidemiologist Sir Michael Marmot, as outlined at length in his 2004 book, *The Status Syndrome*. 'Whitehall I' in 1967 shocked the investigators in its revealing that not the supposedly stressed-out upper managerial men, but men in the lowest employment grades were much more likely to die prematurely (of an array of stress-related diseases). After the follow-up, still vaster 'Whitehall II' in 1985 also came in with results that were every bit as much 'the wrong way round', as it were, Sir Michael had to come up with an explanation. He hypothesised that stress was caused mostly by a sense of lack of control in the job, severely afflicting men in the low grades and not the 'high-flyers'. But those towards the top of the civil service have others above them, who are rather more demanding than is a low-level line manager of his foot soldiers. Upper management hardly is less 'controlled' than 'controlling', for all that Marmot supposes. Worse, he confuses cause and effect. The men at the bottom of the jobs pile likely were there and stayed there because they were in general lowly males, and as such would endure sustained high levels of cortisol. That is, their high levels of cortisol *they brought with them to work*. It's not the work per se that drives up their cortisol. For many, an undemanding job is more a refuge of calm away from 'the rat race' than a wall to bang their heads against. Being low-status, with concomitant high levels of cortisol translating low status into the feeling of being stressed, itself will be experienced in part as a sense of being not 'in control'.

Confirming that Marmot is on the wrong lines, Amanda Sacker, Mel Bartley & others (2000) found that the 'social gradient' (*sic*), as Marmot calls it, applies only to men. The 'Whitehall II' study had expanded to take in women, but Kath Moser, Helena Pugh & Peter Goldblatt (1990), and, separately, Tarana Chandola with others, including Marmot himself (2004), found that not only was the disparity between low and high grade jobs in the impact of stress not apparent with women, but there was an altogether separate, much weaker relationship: according to the women's position *at home* – that is, according to the job grade of *their husbands*, and *not* to their own work grade. This is explained by assortative mating: women marry men corresponding to them in mate-value, and inasmuch as in women there is a relationship between mate-value and stress, as surely there must be to a degree; it hardly can relate to dominance hierarchy because – as I will outline in the next section – dominance hierarchy is not part of human female sociality (that is, social structure & dynamics).

The great contrast between the sexes regarding the stress impact of being within the male-styled work hierarchy is a very neat illustration of what overall is going on regarding male hierarchy as relates to reproductive-suppression. We can describe/label precisely and succinctly: 'Dominance is adaptive stressing and ranking of males in the service of allocating reproduction by differential self-suppressed fertility'. (This encapsulation featured in the title of my first review paper, in 2009.) Dominance hierarchy is the perfect vehicle for the male 'genetic filter' function. [Note that as regards this being an apparent group-level phenomenon, I would refer you to what I said above about the now stale 'individual' versus 'group' selection discussion, which has been superseded and transcended by new understanding. There is no theoretical objection to differential dominance rank being the basis of corresponding relative self-suppression of fertility. Even if there were, the reality of the functioning of dominance hierarchy, cortisol and testosterone, is plain to see, however it may or may not be explained.]

## Section 7

## Hierarchy Proper is Only Ever Amongst Males

This analysis holds assuming that dominance hierarchy is indeed a male rather than a female phenomenon: a male within-sex, and neither a female within-sex nor male-female – cross-sex – phenomenon. If dominance hierarchy is the key mechanism re the male 'genetic filter', then why would it be other than exclusively male-male? Certainly, in the great majority of animal species, dominance hierarchy is observed mainly and most strongly amongst males. Indeed, it would be near ubiquitous in males were it not for the alternative intra-male facilitation of female mate-choice known as lekking (male-male competition for a central physical space, the holding of which entices all females to mate there with only the resident male; this being equivalent to competition for alpha-male status). Formerly (and still usually), dominance hierarchy was thought to be between- as well as within-sex, but it is now clear that this is mistaken. The assumption that all males are dominant to all females stems from failing to understand that juvenile males may play-fight across sex, even with adult females, as rehearsal for future dominance contest. Play-fighting is hardly itself contest for dominance. That dominance can never be inter-sexual is compellingly shown in remarkable neat mammalian experiments by Catherine Dulac (Kimchi & Dulac, 2009; Stowers et al, 2002). It turns out that the core behaviours of dominance and sex are diametrically opposite and controlled as such according to an algorithm whereby the basic default behaviour is not dominance/submission but sexual – specifically male agentic sexual. Dominance/submission behaviour is never engaged without first sexing the other individual encountered, so as to ensure that the appropriate behavioural mode is engaged: specifically that a dominance/submission mode is *not* engaged unless the other individual encountered is of the same sex. This makes it impossible to display dominance (or submission) across sex. In mammalian 'gene knockout' studies, silencing the expression of a gene known as TRP2 renders an individual incapable of sexing any other individuals encountered. This then always prompts engagement in sexual behaviour; conversely, an invariable failure to engage in dominance/submission mode. All other individuals encountered are treated as being female, regardless of the sex of either of the parties! Whether male or female, an individual who is unable to sex another individual he/she encounters, attempts sexual mounting, even if the other is a male. So males and females with the TRP2 gene disabled behave in the very same way – even females actually engage in male sexual behaviour; both to fellow females and to males. Males attempt to mount fellow males as well as females. This starkly reveals the controlling decision rules for any and every individual, from his/her perspective, to be the following algorithm: a default initiation of male-agentic sexual behaviour, *unless* either (a) I am myself male and the other individual is also male, or (b) I am myself female. Then, in the case, (a), engage the dominance/submission behavioural mode; or in the other case, (b), engage the female sexual mode (an arched-back receptive posture to facilitate sexual penetration).

This stunning set of findings is clearly so foundational to behaviour and its neural processing that it must be highly conserved across species (albeit overlaid, as you'd expect, in higher mammals and primates with elaboration of this behaviour and cognition, integration with other cognitive domains, and conflicting with other parts of the 'motivational set' according to set 'decision rules'), so the problem that experiment necessarily for ethical reasons is restricted to relatively lowly mammals – as here, on the mouse – is little obstacle to the wider applicability of the findings. And it is no matter that TRP2 presumably is not the only gene involved. Likely it is one of many integrated in a hierarchy of regulatory and coding genes, and possibly at some remove from the genetic nub but connected as some necessary but hardly sufficient component. So what we might term 'the sex/dominance modes algorithm' could be uncovered by manipulating other genes singly or in combination. The point is that we now know that the algorithm exists as a basic platform of sociality. It makes perfect evolutionary sense given that sex is the most important behaviour, and it is male behaviour that is key in male/female encounters because females can conceive simply by being inert, whereas males must accurately locate the female genital opening and actively penetrate with a penis. Almost as importantly, there has to be a mechanism to stop the inappropriate employment of a dominance-submission mode in what should be a sexual scenario; not just because it would be counter-productive and possibly very damaging, but because of the opportunity costs.

Compelling evidence aside, there is, anyway, inherently no sense to be made of the concept of between-sex dominance when you consider that if what is at issue between the sexes really is dominance, then with inevitably some overlap across sex of physical attributes – at least *some* females are not shorter, weaker or less belligerent than *all* males – there is bound to be at least a few females who would be dominant to the lowliest males. That instead it is always the case that 100% of males supposedly are dominant to females, then this reveals necessarily that something else is going on to divide the sexes that is *not* dominance (or any other basis of hierarchy formation). The opposite, rare, supposed 'female dominance' – all females being dominant, allegedly, to all males – occurring notably in several lemur species, turned out actually to be default male deference to females in giving them priority re feeding (Kappeler, 1993). Again, this is not itself any form of dominance: it's the universal signalling by males of that species of declining to engage in what would not make any sense as a dominance contest.

Another seeming anomaly is in there being some primitive species where there is or appears to be female dominance hierarchy *only*. This is the case for many of the social insects, but there is not really a dominance hierarchy in that it does not apply to the vast majority of females; only to a handful if quite that. There is little in the way of battle to decide between them which one is to be the sole reproducer – the queen. One or two others may be 'held in reserve', you could say. Clearly demarcated though they are with different pheromonal (chemical) signatures, it is questionable, not least through there being so very few individuals involved – in number and, starkly, proportion-wise – for this to be the real McCoy. If it is, then perhaps it's a partial co-option of a male form of sociality to solve a female problem of appointing a sole breeder in 'co-operative breeding' (about which I'll have more to say later). In any case, notwithstanding the absence of male dominance hierarchy, the principle of selection being much greater on the male is maintained. In the case of the honey bee, for example, all males desperately vie with each other in 'scramble competition' as they madly race through the air to be first to catch and mate with the queen. The fitness test for the males here is far greater than that for the females, and so, as ever, selection acts principally on the male.

The main seeming problem for dominance hierarchy befitting a 'genetic filter' function is in the significant number of species where there is female dominance hierarchy as well as that of the male, and where the female dominance hierarchy looks like it might be the real deal. Well, this too turns out to be a figment. As has long been well-known, in many instances of a species exhibiting female dominance hierarchy, the females do not contest for rank; they *inherit* it from their mothers. This is the case for the chimpanzee, for example. While male chimps vie with each other in earnest, female chimps effortlessly come to lord it over other female chimps like blue-blooded aristocrats. Now, this really does look like dominance hierarchy as serving to minimise potentially injurious fighting. The last thing a female 'wants' – the last thing the local reproductive group 'wants' – is anything to compromise her reproductive potential, because the female is the 'limiting factor' in reproduction. This is another way of stating that the females are always set apart to be unhindered in their reproductive role, whereas the males are assigned the task of dealing with accumulated gene replication error.

What, though, about the wider issue of female ranking even when it is *not* inherited? Inheritance of rank appears to be a subset of female dominance hierarchy as it manifests across species, begging the question as to what characterises female dominance hierarchy at root. This was the unanswered question I'd hoped would interest primary researchers with the publication of my very first science review paper I mentioned above, on the theoretical though evidently all too real position here discussed: of dominance hierarchy as functioning to differentially self-suppress reproduction. A startling piece of research in 2015 by Wouter van den Berg, Sander Lamballais & Steven Kushner has given us the answer, which is as profound as I could have guessed: dominance hierarchy in a mammalian model is *male-specific*. By that, they mean that dominance hierarchy proper occurs only amongst males. The ostensible dominance hierarchy of females is a chimera; an artefact of how researchers have gone about trying to record dominance interactions. This is a foundational finding in biology, which in common with other such seminal mechanism is almost certainly remarkably conserved in evolution, so that the same feature is evident stretching back to the evolutionarily truly ancient and forward all the way to humans.

Remember that dominance hierarchy is an epiphenomenon of the constituent individuals, each possessing the neural wherewithal to process 'winner' and/or 'loser' effects. The new study reveals that the key genetic underpinning to the necessary brain circuitry is the SRY gene: the most important gene on the Y chromosome. Only males have a Y chromosome, and therefore females invariably do not have the requisite neural kit, whereas males invariably do. Females can exhibit what may appear to be dominance hierarchy, but the outcome of any contest between a pair of females is not determined or biased by the previous outcomes of encounters, either with the same or other individuals; as would be the case for males. Instead, for females, outcome each time arises anew through mutual assessment there and then, irrespective of past encounters –

even if the very same pair already had sparred before. Although females sometimes may appear superficially to have fully transitive (linear) dominance hierarchy, only males collectively exhibit actual transitive ranking (Van den Berg, Lamballais & Kushner, 2015). Only they have the necessary neural apparatus to implicitly ('non-consciously') compute relative physical and psychological strengths gauged through permutations of conflict histories, so as to then modify future behaviour to engage either more or less, according to the direction and extent of mutual disparities.

The upshot is that how hierarchy usually is envisaged – as simply to reduce and render unnecessary injurious or lethal conflict – in fact applies to females and not to males. It's the female who needs to reduce the possibility of conflict, for (to reiterate) the all too obvious reason that the female is the 'limiting factor' in reproduction, and, therefore, anything that compromises reproduction must be avoided. Females manage this very simply by assessing at each and every encounter with another of their sex if the other has any intrinsic attributes that potentially might make them a handful to have to tackle if ever push came to shove, as it were. Any assessment from previous encounters is not relied upon, so that assessments always are from scratch, presumably to take account of any change in disposition and other factors newly arisen. This is – or at least potentially is – a risk-averse, fail-safe approach for those wary in particular of the potential costs of physical aggression and who don't usually engage in it. For males, not only is there no need to reduce the possibility of conflict, but males actually need, within bounds, to up the ante so as to fully sort themselves according to who really does have 'good genes' and who doesn't. Ranking exacerbates conflict, because it's worth fighting for, and worth fighting in order to improve on, as when individuals do not differ substantially in rank – where the risks of losing against the pay-off of winning are low, when 'transitivity' means that one 'fight' can do for several others, as it were. The seeming intuitively obvious function (particularly of 'transitive') dominance hierarchy of reducing conflict actually is turned on its head.

That it has taken until now to discover just what is dominance hierarchy may seem astonishing. The problem has been a conceptual failure to understand the dominance-submission interaction, through (to reiterate) employing as standard a far too loose merely operational definition, that – as it turns out – fails to distinguish between the phenomenon proper and what is merely ostensible. Mere retreat or even just non-reaction – and in the absence of any signalling of submission – has been assumed to be a dominance 'win' for the party who, in comparison, seemed to stand his/her ground, when this may be, or is more likely to be, no interaction dominance/submission-wise at all.

Though we can clearly see that dominance hierarchy is a male phenomenon, this hardly somehow excludes the female from a major role regarding dominance hierarchy. As I've already mentioned, she makes assessments of males so as to compare their respective genetic qualities to then make a choice of a male to be or not to be her pair-bond or an extra-pair sex partner. She has evolved to accurately detect male rank as an overall quick measure of 'good genes' (to cross-check with other indices). In this way, sexual selection compounds natural selection to weed out deleterious genetic material. So, really, when we talk of the 'genetic filter' ('mutational cleanser') function, it's perhaps mistaken to ascribe it just to the male: given this crucial participation of the female in choosing/eschewing males according to male rank, then this filtration/cleansing is what the whole system of male/female sex is all about. It's a genuine symbiosis between the sexes. The ultimate symbiosis in nature.

## Section 8

## 'Policing' Males Through Prejudice

Careful female mate-choice together with the differential reproductive suppression of males through dominance hierarchy is a gate-keeping exercise to prevent males lacking sufficient 'good genes' from getting access to sex. But how reliable is it? Well, first, can males within the dominance hierarchy easily tell each other apart in terms of relative rank, and in such a way that nobody is misrepresenting where they stand? Can they at least make the thing work amongst themselves?

For dominance hierarchy to function, males have to be able to tell each other's rank pretty well immediately at the start of any encounter, otherwise they would have to start all over again the process of sussing mutual dominance. There must be some sort of signalling – 'honest' signalling. Indeed there is. Apparently, there's more than one system. An initial non-verbal mechanism requires just a mutual glance (Kalma, 1991), followed by monitoring relative dominance constantly and unconsciously, in registering each others' vocal sounds below speech frequencies. Stanford Gregory investigated this thoroughly in the 1990s (Gregory, 1990; Gregory, Webster & Huang, 1993; Gregory & Webster, 1996; etc), finding that the ranking signals in the human voice are within a low-pitched segmented hum under 50Hz. These are used to adjust the pattern of communication according to whether the other male is of higher or lower social status. Compared to how both men and women hear female voices – as sounds, as it's just a matter of activating the brain's auditory region – when men listen to other men's voices a completely different brain region is involved: a structure right at the back of the brain informally known as 'the mind's eye' (Sokhi, Hunter & Wilkinson, 2005). It's here where comparisons are made; especially between oneself and others – and, presumably, it's where the more primitive non-verbal status signalling also is processed. The lower-status party accommodates to the other's speech patterns: automatically changing complex wavelength and amplitude forms to be similar. He also tries to match word use, phrasing, intonation, accent and tone. Correspondingly, the higher-status party monitors the other's accommodation to him, checking if he really is fully indicating sub-dominance. Just how crucial is all of this to male-male communication is easily shown in a laboratory setting where all of the low-frequency signalling can be filtered out of vocal sounds. Social encounters then become very difficult to impossible (Gregory, Dagan & Webster, 1997). Further work on this seems to have revealed, additionally, signalling deference (non-engagement in dominance-submission) to women – in data of interactions between host and guests on the Larry King show, though the authors themselves missed its significance (Gregory & Gallagher, 2002).

So far so good, but like any system where the constituent parties in some respects have an incentive to cheat, male ranking can't be completely reliable; in that however well it works in itself there surely will be some way round it. Yes, lowly males 'internalise' that their rank will not passport them to sex, and their testosterone is reduced to make it less likely that they will try in any really determined fashion to circumvent 'the rules', as it were; even if they were lacking in-built inhibition from so doing. Even so, they may well try to sneak sex, and their efforts and any belligerent nature will serve to drive up their own testosterone levels, and this will be boosted by any success. The attempt to gain sexual access and achieving it 'bootstrap' up together. There is a need, therefore, to have evolved some implicit mechanism to 'police' males – 'policing' being the term usually used in biology (as when insect 'workers' prevent other females from reproducing in competition with the queen).

This easily would be achieved by everyone, male and female, possessing an evolved default prejudicial attitude to males, especially to those whose low-status renders them candidate transgressors. A blanket in-built negative attitude towards low-status males would be simple to evolve, by co-opting the brain circuitry of the primary emotion of disgust. As an alternative possibility to evolving a plain anti-male prejudice, there could be an elaboration of the brain circuitry that enables females to assess males. Females necessarily assess several parallel and overlapping indicators they can cross-check. This 'information redundancy' approach has a better chance of throwing up any anomaly there might be, thus revealing the male's quality (to what extent he has 'good genes') as not what it otherwise seems. The key here would be to look out for what is the exception: the one flaw in the male's display.

Denise Cummins (1996, 2005) recognised the need for a 'violation detection' mechanism to operate specifically regarding dominance-hierarchy (to 'police' low-ranking males), and developed theory and found evidence of just such a mode of reasoning that was implicit (non-conscious and already apparent even in early childhood) applying only in social scenarios. Here, instead of a simple weighing-up of conflicting evidence, reasoning changes to the seeking of exception, so that notwithstanding the weight of evidence in support of a target male individual, a single piece of counter-evidence is all that is needed to decide against him. This is a form of what has been dubbed 'deontic' reasoning: reasoning about obligations, permissions and prohibitions. These are just what apply to individuals by virtue of membership of a dominance hierarchy, depending on and differing according to rank.

Cummins' work is a major part of a substantial literature on 'cheater detection' cognition; this being shown to be activated more in respect of low-status individuals (Cummins, 1999a), specifically *males* of low status (Oda, 1997); and in particular *by* other low-status males (Fiddick & Cummins, 2001). Furthermore, males who are low-status and deemed to 'cheat' are perceived as unattractive (Mehl & Buchner, 2008; Bell & Buchner, 2009). There is a volume of research into the very early emergence of seeking out rule-violation in young children (Cummins, 1996c), who do not display such cognitive facility when it comes simply to ascertaining truth rather than compliance (Harris & Nuñez, 1996; Cummins, 1996b).

This field evokes ideological opposition because it turns upside down the expectation that elite individuals are those who must have 'cheated' (to have acquired their resources), not the lowly (from whom resources supposedly have been stolen). Astonishingly, some 'cheater detection' studies actually have been dismissed on these grounds: that, supposedly, the findings and interpretation are inexplicable by any theoretical position. Impossible to fathom outside biology, perhaps; but not within it. A major problem is the framing in behavioural-economics, which, being a branch of economics, is based on the belief that motivation is always to maximise resources – as if the motivation to gain sexual access didn't exist. There is claim and counter-claim about the memory system involved: whether or not there is greater recognition of the faces of 'cheaters' – whether even this makes sense theoretically (why instead wouldn't we better recall the faces of 'co-operators'?). This is a discussion beyond the scope of the present one, and suffice to say that likely it's resolvable by instead invoking a less specific mode of memory. More problematically, theory here may be awry in that the usual notion of the 'cheater' is in the context of the large body of experimental work seeking the basis of 'altruism', as if no pre-existing biological co-operative sociality could get in the way of the brain working as a supposed general learning device. Effectively, that's an untenable 'blank slate' view, and it is clear that a fundamentally co-operative sociality is very much what evolved early in animal evolution, to be conserved up until and including humans, as is outlined here. The crucial need to take into account already-existing social structure and dynamics is the very issue Cummins addresses as her starting point.

Controversy is also more straightforward and scientific, however. There are issues of interpretation through some difficulties with experimental design. A standard method of testing reasoning is a logic card puzzle known as the 'Wason Selection task', which has been much discussed as to whether the usual inferences taken from its results are justifiable. This has been addressed in part simply by using other means to test reasoning. There continues a debate about whether or not there is a 'cheater detection' *module* (brain circuitry specifically for the job) rather than that identifying 'cheats' is just by more general brain processes. The importance of establishing that there is cognitive 'domain specificity' is that it directly reflects a corresponding specific adaptation, which in turn confirms the biological salience of (in this case) 'cheater detection'. Really, though, the controversy is not a scientific one but a rearguard action by 'blank-slaters', which has flared up more recently in reaction to the case for a 'cheater detection' module being convincingly reaffirmed by fresh research teams entering the fray (Van Lier Revlin & De Neys, 2013; Bonnefon, Hopfensitz & De Neys, 2013); their work endorsed by Cummins (2013). Most to the point, Bonnefon's team additionally found that males are seen as less trustworthy than females.

The topic of biological 'policing' of male sexual access remains rather under-researched to come to a clear understanding, and to progress there needs to be investigation of the neurological basis of the inferred modularity of a 'cheater detection' system. There has to be this kind of confirmation that it's real, and a sorting out of just how it works and how specific it may be.

That 'policing' of males occurs *culturally* could not be more starkly apparent in 'circumcision': male genital mutilation (MGM). There are various extreme forms (including an equivalent of female 'infibulation') traditionally practiced in some cultures, but even partial foreskin removal is a serious indeed mutilation given that it's no mere covering of the penis but a most important feature of it. The foreskin is the part of the penis with the densest set of nerve endings, and is integral to the mechanics of sexual intercourse, so that its removal severely denudes sexual sensitivity (Bronselaer, 2013; Sorrells, 2007; Taylor, Lockwood & Taylor, 1996), thereby reducing inclination for seeking extra-pair sex or responding to an invitation to so indulge. MGM is, then, a most direct cultural extension of 'policing' males. Yet so core to sociality is the 'policing' of males that nobody so much as notices that MGM indeed is 'policing', notwithstanding its being so brutally apparent. Instead, the custom is rationalised; most commonly as a supposed health benefit, when actually the reverse is the case. The foreskin traps anti-microbial secretions against the 'meatus' of the penis, so as to carry away harmful bacteria when it emerges as smegma. For rather understandable reasons 'circumcised' men often deny that their sexual performance is in any sense muted. Or they may be under an illusion through their own more vigorous performance that MGM entails: the relative lack of sensitivity likely leads to more forceful thrusting, which might be (mis)taken to indicate undiminished or even enhanced sexuality, rather than the reduction causing it.

An even more extreme cultural manifestation of 'policing' is to present it as its inverse. The very psychological attitude of this 'control' of males easily becomes its own justification. With our being, in effect, biological machines built on a 'need to know' principle – in other words, we are not even vaguely aware, ultimately, of anything of what we think or behave – then a default attitude of suspicion and derogation towards males (unless and until a male provides evidence to the contrary) we naturally infer is because it is deserved. All kinds of normal behaviour by males may be tendentiously interpreted as actually or potentially 'anti-social' in some way, and males come to be held responsible – blamed – for their own 'policing'. With the whole point of this 'control' of males being to obviate short-cut sexual access to females, then 'policing' of males is flipped to become an assumed inappropriate 'control', not of but *by* males: of *fe*males. This psychological attitude is the basis of how clearly counter-factual ideologies of feminism can arise and hold sway, persisting in deeper entrenchment and being more widely pervasive, despite a mounting strength in converging lines of evidence showing that it has never deserved support.

Enter 'misogyny' (*sic*). This supposed phenomenon is feminist invention flying in the face of the overwhelming amount of evidence and solid theoretical explanation, that in myriad ways the female is deferred to and privileged. Not only is there no evidence for the existence of 'misogyny' (*sic*), but the evidence points instead to the corresponding contempt towards men, misandry, being the real phenomenon – just as would be expected in the translation psychologically into default prejudice, of the biological imperative through the 'genetic filter' function to assess all males and to regard any and every male as defective unless there is a lot of overlapping evidence to the contrary. That in root biology males are obliged to mutually contest in order to earn sexual access, is bound to have major ramifications in psychological and social terms: males are seen as having to earn regard, otherwise they are presumed to be worthless. This never applies to any female. Women would have to behave conspicuously badly to earn disapproval from males; otherwise, invariably they are well regarded. From as young as five years, boys and girls, in both their implicit and explicit attitudes, view females more positively; and this not only remains stable for girls/women, but becomes progressively more pronounced with age for boys right into adulthood (Dunham, Baron & Banaji, 2015). That's fully in line with previous research that anticipated, examined and rejected an ideological claim that the effect would be reduced or become ambivalent in respect of women not in a 'traditional' role (Eagly, Mladinic & Otto, 1991). So it is that assumed 'misogyny' (*sic*) on examination turns out to be antipathy mostly *by other women*; as, for example, the *Demos* think-tank found when in 2016 it looked into the supposed phenomenon of online 'misogyny' (*sic*). The bulk, then, is female within-sex competitiveness manifesting as derogation. The rest is mostly a form of 'policing' of males. It's no surprise, though, that with the 'unfalsifiability' of ideology as the basis of an attempt at theory, together with the evolved negative attitude towards males; that attempt is made to prevent the collapse of the notion of 'misogyny' by claiming that women 'internalise' 'misogyny' (*sic*). This is not only committing the cardinal sin in science of non-parsimony, but the idea that women would somehow have any motivation to accept hatred towards them and then employ it against each other is beyond parody; not that the notion of 'misogyny' (*sic*) itself isn't. The charge of 'misogyny' (*sic*) against males is *itself* the actual abuse and prejudice: misandry.

# SECTION 9

## A SEX-SPECIFIC STRESS MECHANISM UNDERPINS THE MALE DOMINANCE CONTEST

Underpinning (or complementary to) the profound complete distinction between the sexes re hierarchy is stress response mechanism. In this there is further major evidence that it's male sex-specific. Formerly, it was thought or assumed that the way women would deal with stress would be as men do. When at last it was realised that it might be an idea to check, investigation was restricted to crude examination, in a before-and-after stress scenario, of changes to cortisol levels. With refinements of measurement, and experiments to look at how cortisol varied as against levels of testosterone (which women also have), it became very apparent that these key hormones moved in very different directions and patterns – how they rise/fall/remain elevated (or not), etc – according to sex, and that these sex differences also varied according to type of scenario (Mazur, Susman & Edelbrock, 1997; Booth et al, 2006). This was but the start of a whole new research programme elucidating not mere sex difference but sex-dichotomy; sex-specificity.

It is a quite astonishing discovery that the facility to be part of a male hierarchy is grounded in separate, actually sex-specific stress mechanism that females just do not have; right down to genetic and epigenetic expression. [An epigenetic change is one of a standard set of chemical modifications to a gene that is not hereditary but is triggered by some evolutionarily anticipated condition at some point in the course of an individual's development, causing the gene to have a significantly altered effect.] Just as dominance hierarchy for the female entails avoiding contest in order that reproduction is not compromised, so stress for the female likewise seems essentially a problem because of its negative impact on reproduction. Hence females have evolved to escape stressors by easily registering them and experiencing a feeling of being stressed as motivation to escape it; if need be through profound inactivity (as in the major depression which is very much more likely to strike women than men). At the same time, in order to be able to deal with the sort of stress that cannot be escaped, in females there is a dampening down of the impact of stress physiology. The brain physiology behind all this is becoming well understood. Bangasser et al (2010) find that brain receptors for the hormone that initiates the main stress axis, CRF (Corticotrophin Releasing Factor), work in completely different ways according to sex. Females are much more sensitive to low levels and unable to deal with high levels. This means that the female is driven to act to try to alleviate the source of stress and escape it.

The picture in the male is the opposite. There is desensitisation, as well as a much higher threshold to trigger the receptors. This sex-specificity stems from the completely different way that the CRF-receptor works in females (too technical to meaningfully discuss here). The underlying genetic basis of this opposite CRF functioning according to sex is beginning to be revealed (Gilman et al, 2015). Stress for males not only is not the problem it is for females, but it is positively useful, in driving the within-sex competition males require to achieve rank indicating genetic quality in order to gain sexual access to females. What is more, rather than any damage entailed in contesting and maintaining rank being a problem for males (as it would be for females), it actually makes for the 'honest signalling' of genetic quality – the 'keeping them honest' I raised above. Consequently, far from males tending to try to escape stressors, they live with and utilise them, and even, in effect, 'manufacture' stress. To this end, instead of easily registering and experiencing stress, as do females; males have evolved the above-said higher threshold to register stress, but also mechanisms seemingly to attenuate and override stress signals if and when stress becomes less motivational than a distracting nuisance.

Achievement-related stressors drive men, whereas women experience them as negatively stressful. Social rejection spurs men to up their game; women to give up. This is the conclusion of several reviews, e.g., Sordaz & Luna (2012). When reward-seeking is studied, men are found to be motivated by stress when women would shy away; and the brain activation patterning responsible for this sex divide can clearly be identified by fMRI (functional magnetic resonance imaging). Neural activity in two particular sub-regions of the forebrain which extensively feed back to an evolutionarily ancient lower brain structure known as the amygdala, increases in men but decreases in women – a perfectly opposite mechanism according to sex. These findings by Lighthall et al in 2012 confirms much previous work by the same team and by others, directly connecting stress with competitiveness; positively in males and negatively in females.

For some time it had been concluded that stress response diverged sex-typically into what has been widely characterised as male 'fight-or-flight' vis-a-vis female 'tend-and-befriend' modes (Taylor et al, 2000). It was thought that these reflect socialised sex roles, but the explanation clearly would be an evolutionary one: the ancestral male hunter and fighter contrasting with his female gatherer / child-minder counterpart. However, such conceptualisation doesn't go deep enough given where the evidence now points: to the male key SRY gene underpinning the male 'fight-or-flight' response (Lee & Harley, 2012), just as even newer research shows that it underpins male sex-specificity of dominance hierarchy proper, as above outlined. Two decades of intense investigation has led to a paradigm shift to sex-specificity, as Robert-Paul Juster and Sonia Lupien (2012) assert in the title of their paper, 'Sex and gender in stress research: the metamorphosis of a field'. Male versus female stress response in the most important respects is non-overlapping; and this is not regarding merely separate quantitative ranges of what qualitatively is the same mechanism, but actually different neuro-hormonal pathways right down to different genetics and epigenetics according to sex. For example, Yan Wang and his team (2015) used neuro-imaging to examine cerebral blood flow as a result of acute mild stress and indeed found almost nil data overlap, regardless of the type of analysis or classification they used. Stress in men is here associated with increased blood flow in the right pre-frontal cortex and reduction in the left orbito-frontal cortex. Acute stress in women, however, doesn't activate the cortex in any locus. Instead, what is activated are various *sub*-cortical structures – that is, in distinct regional structures in the evolutionarily 'old brain'. Furthermore, unlike with the male response, it is poorly correlated with cortisol levels. Even when system elements appear to be the same – or are dissimilar though corresponding to that of the other sex – then changes in response to stress (such as levels of key hormones and the number/density of their receptors) often are in opposing directions. Most strikingly, overall this produces the contrast of obesity in women as against weight loss in men.

The physiology re stress is highly complex and even the most detailed recent major review, in 2012 by Linda Sterrenburg, shows that there is still a long way to go for it to be fully outlined. Nevertheless, astonishing sex dichotomies already are very well evident, with the promise of much more to come along these lines. Sterrenburg concludes that the limbic regions are activated in response to stress only in males. Only in males too does response to chronic stress get right down to the level of initial gene expression in increasing 'messenger RNA' (the first product of 'reading' – transcribing – a gene) for neuronal CRF (the above-mentioned key hormone initiating the main stress axis) in a key centre within an evolutionarily really ancient core of the brain, the hypothalamus. This is the inverse of the sex-dichotomy when the stress is merely acute; then, only in the female is there the very same change: in response to chronic stress, CRF in females actually declines. This replicated previous findings by others, and indicates that males synthesise CRF to replace all that has been secreted, whereas females simply use up existing CRF and don't replace it. So the male stress response is not just active compared to the passivity of the female's, but is amplified. It's the very opposite of the female pattern which works well as a default strategy to escape the sort of stressors females typically encounter. Neatly, Sterrenburg identifies the actual sex-specific epigenetic changes to the CRF gene – here by all the four epigenetic modes (DNA methylation/ de-methylation and histone acetylation/ de-acetylation) – in different key parts of the limbic system, including the amygdala and the paraventricular nucleus of the hypothalamus. These epigenetic changes in one sex are against an opposite or null change in the other.

Stark contrasts according to sex are particularly well-established with respect to hormones. For females, oxytocin reinforced by oestrogen and other female sex hormones counteracts the negative impact of stress in its being a cortisol antagonist; whereas for males, not only does the absence of female sex hormones preclude an amplification of the effects of oxytocin, but the male anyway has comparatively low levels of oxytocin; and, furthermore, these are depressed by testosterone, which instead promotes (argenine-)vasopressin and thereby an actually amplified stress response (Uvnas-Moberg, 1997; McCarthy, 1995; Jezova et al, 1995; 1996). [Vasopressin has been found to have profoundly different effect according to sex: in males it underpins agonistic (aggressive) behaviour; for females it promotes affiliative responses (Thompson et al 2005).] The impact of stress is further counteracted, uniquely in women, in the inhibition of cortisol secretion by beta-endorphin (Lovallo et al, 2015); and also, as, in 2014, Amandine Minni's team found, through higher levels, compared to men, of Corticosteroid Binding Globulin – CBG, a.k.a. Transcortin, is the protein which binds to and transports cortisol in the bloodstream, resulting in more cortisol becoming tied up and rendered inactive in women. In any case, it is not raised cortisol that in women is responsible for their greater emotional reactivity to stress, but lowering of the female sex hormone estradiol. So it is that Mary Catherine Desoto & Manuel Salinas (2015) in a review and new study showed that for women, neuroticism actually correlates *negatively* with cortisol levels; only for men does cortisol and being neurotic go hand in hand.

More than this very brief overview of sex-specificity re stress, here would be a digression, so the reader is referred to my review paper of last year for an expansion (Moxon, 2015a). I want now to move on to how dominance hierarchy manifests in human development, and then to see what other sociality emanates from it.

# SECTION 10

## HIERARCHY IS CENTRAL TO MALES FROM EARLIEST DEVELOPMENT

Overwhelming evidence reveals that from as soon as very young children begin to be capable of anything that could be considered social interaction, the sexes self-segregate spontaneously, producing a different social world for boys compared to girls – very many studies and reviews, too numerous to cite; the most recent updated review being by Joan & Greg Cook (2015). It occurs certainly by age two or three (Fabes, Martin & Hanish, 2004), if not 18 months, to quickly become the most obvious and well-documented aspect of child development. It becomes so pronounced that for the great majority of children there is little contact with the other sex outside of any forced contact in school. By the age of six, children are more than ten times more likely to interact with same-sex peers. It's the most persistent and reliable developmental phenomenon, continuing right through childhood and adolescent grouping, and across the entire lifespan (Mehta & Strough, 2009). As a prominent researcher in this field, Joyce Benenson, strongly points out, it is central to sex difference in gregariousness (Benenson, Stella & Ferranti, 2015).

It used to be thought that the root cause might be the different sorts of activity the sexes respectively gravitate towards, or by peer influence mediating some sort of 'social conditioning'; but both suppositions have long been shown to be false. Carol Lynn Martin and her collaborators (2013) are the most recent researchers to put such notions to bed. As befits an evolved facility, self-sex-segregation has long been identified as culturally universal (Omark, Omark & Edelman, 1975), and occurs just as strongly in societies that are the nearest to what pertained ancestrally; as Hillary Fouts with Rena Hallam & Swapna Purandare (2013) find in their study of small-scale 'primitive' communities, whether considered actually hierarchical or 'egalitarian'. [Cultural anthropologists have a long track record of being blind to hierarchy when it is not formal and despotic; failing to grasp that ranking, when settled, though ever present takes a back seat, as the necessarily co-operative aspect of hierarchy comes to the fore.] It is also apparent in a range of mammals (Bernstein, Judge & Ruehlmann, 1993). There are all sorts of angles on the phenomenon indicating an evolutionarily highly conserved adaptation. Even strenuous efforts by parents and teachers always fail to reduce same-sex preference for playmates (Rubin & Coplan, 1993). Nor does it even reduce the time spent in same-sex play, because any enforced cross-sex togetherness is made up for by extra same-sex play away from direct adult control (Segal et al, 1987). Judith Rich Harris (1998, 2009) concludes, in her ground-breaking summation of thirty years academic work in developmental psychology, *The Nurture Assumption*, that not the family but the peer group is where children are socialised: by each other, from a very young age, driven by biology.

After self-sex-segregation, the other major common overall conclusion by researchers, as neatly summed up by Amanda Rose & Karen Rudolph (2011), is that: "in contrast, compared to girls, boys interact in larger playgroups with well-defined dominance hierarchies". As with self-segregation by sex, this starts by age three, revealing it to be how sociality initially manifests (as it is first genetically triggered at the age-appropriate juncture), and hardly can be what some external sociality imposes by requiring or eliciting imitation. At three years old there is little difference in the extent to which boys mutually compete in comparison with girls, but henceforth there is a huge divergence, with boys becoming far more competitive and girls far less so (Sutter & Rutzler, 2010). Put another way, boys and girls both affiliate within their respective same-sex grouping but in startlingly different manner – as is powerfully corroborated by the sex-dichotomous effects of oxytocin, very well-known as the principal hormone underpinning affiliative behaviour: boosting co-operation in women yet competitiveness in men (Fischer-Shofty, Levkovitz & Shamay-Tsoory, 2012). The large-group hierarchical structure and dynamics of even infant males is very much at the heart of Judy Chu's book, *When Boys Become Boys* (2014). Human male hierarchy is (as is well-known) so well attested by studies starting long ago, that it is needless to list them. This may partly explain why it is so hard to find recent papers, but the major reason seems to be political sensibilities and intrusion to consider the sexes to be interchangeable instead of looking at sociality according to sex. As regards sociality research in general; in 2003, Anne Sebanc's team bemoaned: "peer group studies often do not analyze gender, or occasionally do not report the gender differences they find". Sure enough, looking more widely at sociality research, a very well-known account – the 1998 book, *Peer Power: Preadolescent Culture and Identity*, by Peter & Patricia Adler – ignores or only hints at sex differences; describing 'cliques' as if they are also how boys socially organise, and confusing them with 'crowds'. Studies are almost always heavily predicated by ideological constructs, usually being 'applied' investigations, into such as substance abuse, bullying, or educational attainment. Recently, there have been efforts to cut across peer grouping to look only at what can be considered irrespective of sex, by way of indirect denial of the sex dichotomies long all too obvious.

The seminal research was done some time ago. Regarding boys (and boys vis-a-vis girls), I'll summarise in a paragraph the overall thrust of the findings by those who have ventured; notably the early pioneer, Dexter Dunphy (1963), whose work on adolescent group stages, in 2000 was endorsed by Jennifer Connolly, Wyndol Furman & Roman Konarski. The need to address how friendships are embedded (or not) in group structures in particular was addressed by Kathryn Urberg and her collaborators (Serdar Degirmencioglu and others) through the 1990s (Urberg, 1992; Urberg, Degirmencioglu, Tolson & Halliday-Scher, 1995; Urberg, Degirmenciogl, Tolson & Halliday-Scher, 2000; Degirmencioglu, Urberg, Tolson & Richard 1998), and in the noughties by Bradford Brown & Christa Klute (2003, 2008).

Boys' friendships are embedded within hierarchy: they are secondary, really, in importance compared to ranking. So boys and men perceive themselves in terms of their own ranking(s) and see all other ranks as being collectively their peer group. From this strong form of acquaintanceship may derive friendships, but these always stay couched within the whole group from which they arose. Same-sex association by both sexes persists into and through adulthood, albeit that mixed-sex grouping emerges in adolescence to facilitate pairing-off. High 'mate value' individuals of both sexes come together to form a super-group in which dating takes place considerably earlier than for everyone else. These individuals have more romantic attachments and have sex at a younger age. This elite is, to an extent, then imitated by the rest, though grouping still stays mainly same-sex as 'crowds' are formed. That these have little function other than to facilitate pairing-off is revealed in that as soon as pairing more generally gets under-way, 'crowds' start to dissolve. Other than with their opposite-sex pair-bond partners, the sexes return to their same-sex affiliation, which grows stronger still in late life, with friendship for most becoming exclusively same-sex.

Overall, then, for males, hierarchy is the underlying organisational principle from the off and remains so right to the end. It may seem at times weakly so, but not when you consider – as is very well apparent when you think about it – that boys/men can be members of a number of parallel, overlapping and nested hierarchies, and which can be on any scale.

## SECTION 11

## BOYS / MEN GROUP ALL-INCLUSIVELY BEYOND THEIR HIERARCHY

Yet hierarchy is not the only form of sociality of which males partake. What is most nearly contiguous with male dominance hierarchy is how males group. A dominance hierarchy is itself a group, of course: an all-inclusive, all-male group. But dominance hierarchy is neither the only sort of grouping nor the only all-inclusive grouping to which males belong. And males don't belong only to groups comprising only males. A confusion arises here from sociology and social psychology, where the term for implicit psychologically salient grouping, 'in-group', is usually taken to mean a collection of people with a major attribute in common; most especially that the constituent individuals are all of the same sex. This is always or at least usually what is meant by 'male in-group', as if males see themselves only as associating with other males. They don't. The all-inclusive sense of grouping that males feel regarding hierarchy is easily and naturally further extendable to encompass anyone and everyone with whom, through that hierarchy, a male is associated – not least females (plus any children). Research reveals that men's sense of their 'in-group', unlike for women, shows *no same-sex preference* (Goodwin & Rudman, 2004). Even in a newly formed group with the most trivial basis of mutual association (in the jargon, a 'minimal grouping' condition), of individuals randomly put together in pairs for experiments on grouping in psychology labs, men are not only more co-operative than are women; but, in marked contrast to women, this does not depend on any expectation of the other party reciprocating (Yamagishi & Mifune, 2009). This allows the male 'in-group' to become the entire community. Ancestrally, this would be the small-scale tribal sub-community – the travelling group, which, upon the advent of permanent settlement, became the village – into which the male was born and would have spent his whole life. Expressed in a contemporary 'mega-society' context, this could be any 'symbolic' community (Maddux & Brewer, 2005), even if largely abstract, transient, nested, etc; such as the work team and/or the entire workplace, the school year-group and/or the class, the university department and/or everyone on a national student demo ...

This male all-inclusiveness to produce a whole male-female community where males collectively feel protective towards females, is necessary because ancestrally – and as is still to be seen in extant 'forager'/hunter-gatherer societies – the male relatives and partners of a group of females were at risk of aggression from males of another community ('out-group' males, as we might call them). The psychological adaptation to deal with this is readily apparent in experimentation. Drew Bailey & others (2012) find that only males (never females) are more co-operative in the face of an out-group threat. Ancestrally, as today in many 'primitive' societies, neighbouring males sought to acquire 'foreign' females as 'brides' or for illicit or extra-pair sex that within their own community would have been unavailable or would result in punishment by the girl's relatives. 'In-group' males, being relatives and partners of the women, would have had a strong desire to prevent this, and so were obliged to defend their co-resident females en bloc. Any confrontation clearly had the potential to escalate to a deadly fight, with resident males needing to act as a coalition, which they readily would have done in that males are always in a coalition as their dominance hierarchy. 'Out-group' males would have raided to kill males and 'take over' their females, even to the extent of the destruction of the community, if they succeeded in despatching all of the adult males. This scenario would have led to an evolved facility for close cooperation both in raiding and community defence against raiders, which is the foundation of warfare and why it persists to this day and always will do.

Just as in warfare today, 'out-group' males would not have been a threat per se to the community's females, in that in the overall picture females actually could have benefited from them. As bold raiders, they were likely to be considered by 'in-group' females as being as high as or still higher in mate-value than their own males; and, therefore, in having superior complements of 'good genes', they may be preferable as mates – either as an extra-pair sex or pair-bond partner ('marriage by capture'). A shadow of this reality is evident in the very different content of paranoid delusions and dreams according to sex. Men's feature groups of unfriendly male strangers, as you'd expect; but women's don't. Instead, they feature familiar women. Very few women psychiatric patients have delusions about being sexually coerced (Zolotova & Brune, 2005; Walston, David & Charlton, 1998). Evidently this was not a prominent ancestral fear. The ancestral reality seems to explain the usual female response regularly attested to by both victims and perpetrators of 'stranger rape', of the victim becoming limp and 'freezing'. It's the persistence of what ancestrally was adaptive: to shut down emotional and physical resistance in women should they encounter raiding males. The context today usually is the near exactly corresponding one of a war theatre, where the female victims are 'out-group' to the 'enemy' males; but there is also an 'in-group'/'out-group' boundary in the case of the 'stranger' rapist and his quarry. It's much more than the need for a crossing of any sort of social boundary just so that the rapist can feel confident of his anonymity. The frequency of an ethnic divide points to a profound 'in-group'/'out-group' distinction being a prerequisite for a male to be sufficiently disinhibited to consider perpetrating blatant sexual coercion – as in the mass sexual assaults and rapes by thousands of ethnically distinct migrants in the centres of major German cities on New Year's Eve 2015.

Really, then, the ancestral raiding scenario is an extension of male-male competition for rank (and, in turn, their sexual selection by females), where, instead of being within-group, the contest is *between*-group. Correspondingly, it's an extension of 'genetic filter' functioning; part and parcel of it.

# SECTION 12

## How Women's Sociality Arises from Men's: Women 'Marry Out'

Having fleshed out male sociality from the male 'genetic filter' function, it's time to look at how female sociality fits with this. Already this has been more than just touched on in the researched contrast with male sociality discovered in the studies cited above. Just as would be anticipated, girls'/women's social structure/dynamics evolved very differently: in a narrow way concerning reproduction; co-operating with other girls/women in rehearsal for and then in actual mutual child and mother support. So far so obvious; what is not so is why the bonding involved is as strong as it is.

The reason that such close cooperation ancestrally was important, was not only because women had to continue gathering whilst their males were away hunting, but because their consanguineal kin – their blood relatives – were not available. They remained back in the woman's community of birth, from where, upon marriage, the woman moved away to her husband's community. This pattern of female 'marrying out' stems indirectly from the male sociality required re the 'genetic filter'. Allow me to elucidate.

The cohesion amongst males of being, from early childhood, ranked within an all-inclusive hierarchy of males who grow up together to form an enduring coalition, entails males being tied to the place where they were born. Ancestrally, even if a male wanted to break with all those he knew and leave his natal community, it would have been very difficult indeed for him to enter another, to then try to establish rank from scratch. It's unlikely he'd survive on his own approaching much further than the periphery of a foreign group's territorial range. A coalition of male defenders likely would intercept the interloper and if not kill him, then cause him injury, which would in effect be a death sentence deferred. Consequently, men were tied down to do or die together with a moderate or small sized group of males to whom they would have felt fairly well bonded. The tight geographical rooting of males generation after generation then creates a major problem in the local gene pool of undoing what together the recombination of genes and separation of mating types in sex otherwise would counteract – the accumulation of deleterious genetic material – because of 'in-breeding'. If all or most marriage were to be amongst locals, then their close genetic similarity would lead to a great increase in the prevalence of harmful recessive alleles (variant half-genes) pairing up in offspring (as with a 'homozygous' gene), so that instead of being overridden by dominant, non-harmful alleles (as in a 'heterozygous' gene), they would be unmasked and thereby fully expressed. However, inter-marriage of relatives would occur only if both males *and* females remain on the home turf; and, ancestrally, the two sexes didn't 'want' to remain on the same turf. The problem of in-breeding was avoided by the evolution of implicit psychological incest-avoidance. Though the actual mechanism as yet is not clear, it's very evident in humans (e.g., recently, Marcinkowska, Moore & Rantala, 2013; Fessler & Navarrete, 2004). Known for the past century as the 'Westermarck effect', it's apparent when opposite-sex individuals grow up together within the same family or other very close existence, and then upon reaching sexual maturity find they have no mutual sexual interest. (The famous example of children in Israeli kibbutzim has been disputed, but there are many studies from several angles providing clear support for the 'Westermarck effect'.) The ancestral communal village would have lacked the private space of the modern world and would have been, by our standards, a radically communal existence. For everyone to stay put hardly was an option, then.

Some form of exogamy ('marrying out') is necessary to avoid what otherwise would be a gathering genetic disaster of in-breeding. It has long been established in ethology (the study of animal behaviour) that in every sexually reproducing species, not least all primates, at least one sex disperses. [It is not a requirement that every individual of the dispersing sex does so. As with any behaviour, there will always be motivational conflicts resulting in some individuals not conforming to the norm. There may even be whole communities or even a culture or two bucking the overall trend to practice the inverse. A strong tendency suffices to head off the problems of in-breeding.] With males tied to their natal community, then there has to be *female* exogamy. So it is that just as it is for most of our primate relatives, female exogamy is very much the norm and (in normal conditions) a human universal characteristic. The human species is said to be 'patrilocal' – fathers stay put (Murdock 1967; Korotayev, 2003). A tendency towards matrilocality becomes evident only if male mortality is exceptionally high. Patrilocality was important throughout the great bulk of the time-frame of human evolution, when community had to be small-scale to remain ecologically viable. We may not perceive this sex-dichotomous pattern in our contemporary developed-world mega-settlements, where in-breeding is not an issue when finding a partner just a street or two away effectively is to 'marry out' in ancestral terms (that is, there would be a genetic mix of quite different genomes despite very close geographical proximity).

The usual ancestral female 'marrying out' of the natal community would have set up a major protracted selection pressure on women. The consequence of female exogamy for a woman was that from a situation in her natal community of solid kin support, she suddenly found herself in her new home upon marriage without any. The only prospect would have been to cultivate the far less reliable affinal relatives ('in-laws') to replace her consanguineal (blood; that is, actual) ones. And close affiliation was necessary to be able to both forage and otherwise fend for herself while at the same time ensuring care for her children. Just as in contemporary 'primitive' societies, women would have shared childcare. Husbands/fathers would not have made themselves available as childminders – and neither, originally, did they significantly provision the wife/mother (the reasons for which will be set out in the discussion below on pair-bonding). All too often they would be away on long hunting expeditions, or defending against raiding – or raiding themselves. With anyway by some estimates ancestrally (as for some remote hunter-gatherer tribes today) up to a 50% or greater likelihood of death at another man's hands, as well as the possibility of hunting accidents; then the husband hardly could be relied upon even to be there for some of the time; and this would become factored in to evolved behaviour.

It was imperative, then, for a woman to form an alliance with some females who, hitherto, were complete strangers, but who could be bonded to with sufficient strength to be fully trustworthy with her children (and, reciprocally, who could trust her with theirs), and to provide support for herself at crucial times – in later gestation, childbirth, post-partum recovery, and (through the heavy nutritional demands of) lactation. As a result, rather than participating in all-embracing loose hierarchies, which at best would be to pointlessly mimic men and boys; girls and women evolved instead to group in a near opposite fashion. Each individual forms a small idiosyncratic close-bonded little chain or cluster of female (non-sexual) intimates, which (usually) is unique to her. For want of generally agreed terms, I refer to these as, singly, the particular female's own 'personal network', and, collectively, for the matrix of all of these overlapping chains and clusters, 'the female personal network'. For girls and women the sense of 'group' is not something that is shared. The choice of each and every reciprocal bond had to be fairly careful: selective. And there has to be a ruthlessness in being prepared to dump anyone who slips from complete personal trustworthiness. So it is that girls and women have such a distinctive mode of social structure and dynamics, completely different to that of males. Girls in effect rehearse how in the future they will have to organise their social lives. They have a dry run within their natal community as children and adolescents.

Whereas males see themselves first as part of the group and only secondarily in terms of friendship ties, for females there are only friendship ties: their own particular friendship cluster *is* their 'group'. This radical sex dichotomy showed up in the broadest terms when, in 2013, Ilse Lindenlaub & Anja Prummer looked at whole networks: males have more friends in a sparser network; women have fewer friends but in a denser network. The very same was found by Michael Szell & Stefan Thurner (2013). Ditto Tamas David-Barrett and co (2015), when they carried out cross-cultural research they titled in conclusion: *Women Favour Dyadic Relationships, but Men Prefer Clubs*. It's been best illustrated in a study (already cited, above) of university students by William Maddux & Marilyn Brewer (2005). A man automatically sees his department or year group, etc – any symbolic agglomeration – as his group, whereas a woman cuts right across such symbolic boundaries, and, through a friend, across a symbolic boundary – even beyond the college – to identify, indirectly, more with her friend's friend (who may be someone she's never met) than with anyone within the symbolic boundary yet outside of her 'personal network'. Trust in these sort of strangers is far easier for a man: in this example scenario, anyone and everyone from his own college. Inadvertently this seems also to have been unknowingly uncovered, in 2013, by Agnieszka Golec de Zavala, Aleksandra Cichocka & Michał Bilewicz in their series of five studies purporting to show a negative attitude towards the 'out-group' when, in place of a positive 'in-group' regard, there is a lack of identity through "unacknowledged doubts about the group's greatness" and a sense of group only through a constant need for validation by others of what anyway is an over-blown view of oneself that they term "collective narcissism". The problem with their conclusion is that sampling was overwhelmingly of females, yet it was assumed that they would see as their 'in-group' the sort of symbolic grouping only males would thus recognise. The upshot is that what was demonstrated was not 'out-group' derogation generalisable across sex, but negative attitude or derogation by females; likely towards everyone bar those in each female's own 'personal network': everyone else within the symbolic groupings that to men would be 'in-group' members.

So the 'personal network' a girl/woman forms is not, as it would be for males, subsumable in a much wider and all-inclusive grouping (the male dominance hierarchy < male-female 'in-group'). The female 'personal network' *is* her 'in-group'. For women, the sociological / social psychological conceptualisation of 'in-group' as same-sex is much closer to the reality: women have a four-fold same-sex preference regarding prospective fellow group members (Goodwin &

Rudman, 2004) – in contrast to males (as I cited, above) who make no distinction between male and female when it comes to grouping beyond hierarchy. So not only is the root of non-sexual (that is, non-reproductive) affiliation markedly contrasting according to sex, but whereas males expand still further out from what already is notably all-inclusive to identify their 'in-group', females just stay with their 'personal network'. Pamela Popielarz (1999) finds that when left free to associate with whom they will, women show much greater homophily (strong gravitation towards others who are the same as yourself) and homogeneity, so that not only do women rather than men belong to sex-segregated wider groups, but that these groups restrict membership to fellow women of the same age, education, and marital & work status.

To reiterate the flip-side to this: female personal networking has to be selective because at stake is the well-being and safety of a woman's reproductive output; current and potential. Anyone not 'in' is very much 'out' – those not 'with us' are 'against us'. In any case, beneath co-operation there is an underpinning default of competition: females obviously are going to be highly competitive over mates; both in acquiring and maintaining them. For example, co-wives in polygynous marriages are highly fractious whilst in their reproductive years (Jankowiak, Sudakov & Wilreker, 2005). That there is profound female-female competition in acquiring pair-bond partners, I will detail in a later section. The upshot is that female 'in-grouping' is anything but the all-inclusive affair it is for males, being marked by its *ex*clusivity. Joyce Benenson (2013) concludes as in her paper's title: *Social Exclusion: More Important to Human Females Than Males*. In their series of studies, Benenson's team find that "females are more willing than males to socially exclude a temporary ally ... report more actual incidents of social exclusion than males do ... perceive cues revealing social exclusion more rapidly than males do …. (and their) heart rate increases more than males' in response to social exclusion. Together, results indicate that social exclusion is a strategy well-tailored to human females' social structure". Many researchers, such as Marjorie Goodwin (2002), concur that female (but not male) in-grouping is exclusionary.

With 'female personal networking' being not only exclusionary towards males but also to all other females, then whereas the male style of sociality can be said to be civic; the female equivalent could be said to be nepotistic. There are male and female poles within community, where the sexes respectively are 'designed', as it were, to operate. It is not true to say that any society is 'male-dominated'. Females are in full control of their own sociality, regarding which males have no influence; but the converse does not hold. Females have considerable influence on male sociality, being able to easily manipulate males institutionally to behave at their behest – even so far as to successfully convince males that it is their public duty to be at least partly replaced by them! Even local institutions, that being institutions might automatically be considered men's domains because of the male civic role, actually can be female domains, and often purely so. From early last century, the key 'club' in many an English village has been *The Women's Institute*, and in many an English town, *The Townswomen's Guild*. In Italy – where the family conspicuously is ruled by the matriarch – bar the priest, locally the church is an overwhelmingly female institution. It is a politicised and ignorant assertion that if there is a minority of women at the pinnacle of civic life then demonstrably women must be lacking in 'power', or that they must be victims of negative discrimination. That makes no more sense than to claim that any and every society is 'female-dominated' in that males don't get a look-in anywhere away from the civic end of community and at or towards what may be called the extended domestic form of collective existence.

Female sociality, even when all involved are non-kin, looks somewhat like a within-family dynamic. 'Female personal network' in some lights seems like an extension of family relationships, almost as if girls try to recreate their family background anew – to rehearse creating their own family in the near future? – when within their peer group. We could test this if for a long period of time we completely isolated a large number of females away from any contact at all with males. An impossible experiment to mount, there is a de facto experiment of just this male-less environment for females: women's prisons. And because these institutions provided such a radical social 'experiment' there has been no shortage of researchers conducting studies of the social interactions therein. 'Recreating' the family is exactly the social pattern found inside female prisons, whether in the First or Third World, and whether this was before or after the social changes ensuing after the 1960s (Colarelli, Spranger & Hechanova, 2006; Ireland, 1999; Onojeharho & Bloom, 1986; Giallombardo, 1966; Ward & Kassebaum, 1965). Women prisoners, in the absence of males, faithfully reproduce the variety of intra-familial relationships, even to the extent of some women being obliged to take on what would be male roles 'on the outside'.

# Section 13

## The 'Queen Bee' Is The Rainy-Day Default Sole Breeder

The exclusionary nature of female sociality is so striking that it's surely more than just taking care to associate only with females who would seem to be good co-mother ('allomother', in the jargon) material; in the case of girls, to rehearse for this in the future. It's the form of exclusion and the way it's done that is interesting. The females who are marginalised tend to be those who can be picked on for their relative low fertility; that is, they display facets indicating low mate-value, which can be latched on to as being unattractive and ripe for derogation. Famously, this is in terms of sexual propriety – the regular 'ho' and 'slut' jibes. On the face of it, this looks like a means of trying to dissuade males from considering the excluded girls as potential pair-bond partners by planting seeds of doubt as to their likely fidelity; that is, that they are unlikely to be faithful. At the same time, high-fertility females are concentrated in a 'top clique', which, on the same lines, looks like a magnet for high-status males. But is all this done with males 'in mind', as it were; or is there some other basis?

/ Strides have been made in understanding, less in the formal research of academia (where age cohorts of children and adolescents increasingly have been regarded as if they were unisexual) than in the concrete world of 'parenting education'. Parents feel a very strong need to know the social reality of their daughters' lives so that they can keep them safe and smooth their path. *Queen Bees & Wannabes: Helping Your Daughter to Survive Cliques, Gossip, Boyfriends, and Other Realities of Adolescence* was the book that revolutionised how parents understood the lives of their daughters. When Rosalind Wiseman in 2002 first published, it was explosive because what she outlined was immediately recognised as the reality by parents and daughters alike – well, most of all by daughters, as they were in the thick of it at the time. Ditto a parallel book, also first out in 2002: Rachel Simmons' *Odd Girl Out: The Hidden Culture Of Aggression in Girls*. *Queen Bees* spawned the famous film, *Mean Girls*, and derivatively the book, *The Mean Girl Motive: Negotiating Power and Femininity*, by Nicole Landry (2008), based on her extensive interviewing of girls. Landry concludes that the chief currency of 'popularity' is femininity: as indicated by its key aspects, such as white skin, a thin body type, and "good hair"; and that all girls constantly are scrutinised for the femininity of their appearance and behaviour. Whereas popular girls are mean, all other girls are the opposite in being nice as the way to ingratiate themselves and avoid wrath. Wiseman's 2009 updated edition of *Queen Bees* provides more concrete detail regarding the different roles girls play in and outside of 'cliques'.

Other than the 'queen', all girls to varying extent are the 'wannabes'. There is the queen's 'sidekick' (lieutenant and under-study), but everyone else is an also-ran (my term), including the other girls in the 'top clique', who are played off one against the other in a game to keep the 'queen' in that position. A girl can end up in the 'top clique' by acting as a gossip gate-keeper: the 'banker' role. The obvious 'wannabe' is the 'pleaser', in supporting the 'queen' and the 'sidekick' in everything, not least doing the more unpleasant bidding of the 'queen'; whilst at the same time taking pains not to be seen as trying too hard, in case this is seen to be an attempt to usurp the 'queen'. Adhering not quite so obsequiously to the 'queen', the 'torn bystander' tries to ride the conflicts between others. Then there is the 'floater', who cultivates friendship in different groups, but (as with the 'pleaser') is careful not to be considered threatening to the 'queen'. Any girl in any of these roles easily can slip, through being seen – however unfairly – to challenge the 'queen', to join the other 'targets' (mainly relatively unfeminine girls); the victims everyone tries to avoid becoming themselves. [And yes, this isn't a classification arrived at with scientific rigour, but it beats aggregating across sex to deny that girls scheme amongst themselves in this manner.]

Evidently, this is a social system built around one individual. The 'queen' designation is apposite. The 'queen bee' hardly could be more obviously the human equivalent of just as her name indicates in biology: the female sole reproducer. This is the system in the many mammal species dubbed 'co-operative breeding', where there is a very heavy skew in reproductive output, usually pretty well 100% to just the one female; with all the other adult females being allomothers. Not that the skew has to be 100% or anything like. By reason of allomothering being so evident for humans, the prominent demography/reproduction researchers Ruth Mace and Rebecca Sear (2005) conclude, albeit in controversial exaggeration, that we should be considered a 'co-operative breeding' species. In extremis, it's a system that entails all other females bar the sole female reproducer being reproductively suppressed at least to some degree, which can be achieved directly by the stress caused in the harsh and unpredictable behaviour of the sole reproducer towards them. The only way that other females then can reproduce themselves is to move outside of their community of birth. So this system fits perfectly with the imperative of female exogamy in giving females a distinct push to leave and 'marry out'. Not that this is its function, though. 'Co-operative breeding' counters the possibility of local extinction in times of severe ecological stress. In some species this can be 'obligatory' – invariable – because the environment is harsh enough always to mean there's a distinct risk of local extinction. The meerkat is a good and (after the wonderfully revealing *Meerkat Manor* TV series) now the best-known example, living as it does in desert conditions. But in some species it is 'facultative' – it kicks in only when it is needed. For the human case, this previously has been suggested, in 2009 by Marco Del Giudice. With humans, presumably it would come into play only occasionally: at times of serious ecological stress. It's now known that women have evolved to eschew pair-bonding in reaction to conditions inauspicious for reproduction (Reeve, Kelly & Welling, 2016); the sex-specific mechanisms underpinning which have already been unravelled (Toufexis et al, 2013). At such a time, the problem of in-breeding recedes to irrelevance. There is no issue of in-bred fertility depression to deal with if there is no surviving local population. In focusing reproduction narrowly on only the very highest mate-value female (and corresponding male), then there would be a combination of maximum fitness and minimum resource consumption, to provide the best shot to try to pull through. The most fertile female monopolises reproduction, making use of other females to support her in providing care of her infants and obtaining food – which they require less of themselves, owing to their not gestating or lactating, as they would be if they too were reproducing.

The irony here is that the support from other females is obtained after being harassed by the very female who gets this support; with the harassment itself being not the least cause of their reproduction being suppressed. With the need of offspring for support evoking deep-seated adaptive behaviours that are inherently satisfying to perform, then allomothering for non-reproducing females genuinely is a consolation activity. It's the residual function that is the nearest that the women will get to being mothers of their own offspring.

That the human 'queen bee' appears to be the default sole female reproducer, should a scenario arise that is so critical that local extinction is in the offing ….. anyone not familiar with 'co-operative breeding' in biology (and biology generally) might find fantastic. Others may grant that it seems and likely is real enough, but that it must be so ancestral as to be vestigial (a vestige of the evolutionary past, now withered from non-use, and, being no longer adaptive, a behavioural equivalent of the classic case in physical structure of the appendix). Some may concede that the all too real imperatives of human female social existence indicate otherwise; at least for a rarefied handful of girls. Nonetheless, albeit that all girls are impacted by these shenanigans, for most girls their main social experience is being part of a tight female friendship chain/cluster, which apparently – to reiterate – is rehearsal for female-female bonding in a mutual childcare and mother-support network upon 'marrying out'.

# Section 14

## Pair-Bonding Serves Women, but Not Through Men being Providers

Readily apparent though female sociality as a child/mother support network would be from looking at how women interact in anything like a 'traditional' working class neighbourhood, we have lost sight of this. Our social mobility has radically broken down community, obliging the state to take over what were previously small-community childcare functions; and then there is (as we shall see) our poor, indeed radically mistaken understanding of the basis of human pair-bonding – the various formal and informal arrangements of 'marriage', that being a human cultural universal (albeit with an average duration of only four years) (Fisher, 1989, 1994) is an encoding of an adaptive bond between the sexes. [Pair-bonding, in all species exhibiting it, is a product of evolution, and for closely related species such as primates it will have a common adaptive basis, the understanding of which is a major key to the wider understanding of the sexes and their respective socialities.] The importance of 'female personal networking' has been sidelined through the assumption that ancestrally the mother and her children were supported most especially by the husband/father, with any other support being secondary; but that's a myopia born of a perspective from modern cultures in 'developed' nations where the nuclear rather than the extended family is the basic unit of community. As I've just explained, human female social psychology is based in reciprocal child (and mother) support.

The overall conclusion of recent major overviews of research is that human pair-bonding evolved for quite different reasons to those commonly supposed. The male role in pair-bonding is not one of provisioning. To the extent it has become so is a latter-day change in the wake of the evolved basis of pair-bonding. Provisioning may itself have little if any evolutionary basis. More to the point, there is scant evidence of much in the way of provisioning by males that makes a substantive difference. Never mind provisioning, whether or not a father is even present, comprehensive data, extensively reviewed in 2008 by Rebecca Sear and Ruth Mace, shows almost nil impact on child survival. For all pair-bonding species, we now know that male provisioning *post-dates* the evolution of pair-bonding (Brotherton & Komers, 2003), and specifically regarding humans, Bernard Chapais (2008) in providing easily the most comprehensive – the definitive – recent review of the origins of pair-bonding, arrives at the same conclusion. Re-stating and elaborating his arguments in 2011, Chapais sees human pair-bonding as "a *pre-adaptation* for the evolution of parental cooperation in the provisioning of … children". Concurring in a review paper also of 2011, David Geary and Drew Bailey trace the evolutionary path back through primates to polygyny (literally, 'many-female': where some males have simultaneous multiple pair-bonds), which only then gave rise to provisioning by males. The other important major recent review is that in 2006 by Jeffrey Winking, who finds that not provisioning but 'mate-guarding' (see below) is the basis of human pair-bonding.

Yet there is an obvious basis of pair-bonding entirely overlooked by theorists: to solve the problem for women that female fertility falls off a cliff with age (and also the impact on the body of pregnancy and childbirth). Perhaps the most vivid illustration of this reality is what prostitutes charge according to their age: a new study has found that a twenty-year-old can charge fully twice as much as a 30-year old (Sohn, 2016). There are huge implications of this. If when very young (at or near the peak of fertility, shortly after puberty), through the fertility indicators of youth and beauty that at that time she possesses, a female can attract a male partner of corresponding mate-value and secure him over a lengthy period; then she can have successive children with the same complement of 'good genes' at each successive conception. She can, in effect, *project forwards* in time her peak of fertility. Of course, the female alternatively could reproduce successively by finding a partner anew for each subsequent conception, but she faces a significant downside doing it that way. Her offspring likely would be of decreasing genetic quality, in line with the progressively poorer male genetic complement as the mate-values of the best men she is able to acquire fall with her advancing years (and the effects on her body of childbirth). Ideally, a woman requires a man to be a pair-bonded partner beyond the first time they conceive, until after gestation, birth and breast-feeding, right through the re-commencement of cycling and up to when she again conceives. This would ensure that *two* offspring are fathered by the same male. We would expect, therefore, that pair-bonding would evolve to last at least this long. Actually, this might be long enough, given the other conflicting imperatives in life that might arise after such an elapse of time. An evolved pair-bond to usually endure for a few years beyond this could be counter-productive. In any case, other ways people come to feel close to each other usually kick in when you have got so used to someone being always there. The surprisingly short average duration of four years found by Helen Fisher now makes sense: but Fisher didn't take account of the period of informal, prior to formal pair-bonding.

Note that though over the course of the duration of the pair-bond the female partner experiences a decline with age in mate-value – obviously so in her diminishing physical attractiveness; there is no corresponding fall in the mate-value of the male partner. Unlike fertility, 'good genes' don't change – not appreciably. Genes of male sperm can deteriorate as the male gets much older, because of mutations in the cells producing sperm; but this is as nothing compared to the accelerating failure rate of a woman's eggs right from when she first attains sexual maturity – most fertilised ova don't properly implant (are imperceptibly 'miscarried') even in the youngest women. Unlike men, who constantly produce anew vast numbers of their sex cells (sperm), women produce a very limited number of theirs (eggs) and then have to store them. With the deterioration in storage, and in the absence of the sort of relentless selection pressure that any single sperm has gone through to even get a sniff at being the one to achieve fertilisation; a woman's egg is more than likely to have significant defects that become apparent shortly after it is fertilised. The resulting zygote then either fails to develop properly or never even gets implanted. It's not long before the failure rate so much exceeds the success rate that the woman becomes effectively infertile.

A male's 'good genes' are revealed in status (male dominance or prestige rank), which usually increases over time with cumulative outcomes of male-male competition. Some males do of course 'flat-line' or actually fall in status, but this propensity usually will be evident beforehand in the mate-value criteria females scrutinise, leaving such males of little interest to females. So it is that pair-bonding can be considered as the intersection of very different life-history trajectories in terms of mate-value according to sex. Bluntly, a woman is a depreciating asset, whereas a man is an appreciating one. To be precise and succinct … if wordily pretentious: there is sex-dichotomous mate-value trajectory. This major divergence over time between women and men in terms of attractiveness, provides a clear basis for pair-bonding in the female interest.

Notwithstanding this phenomenon being a staple of common understanding, the received wisdom is that pair-bonding – not just in the human case but across species generally – functions as male proprietorial control of female sexuality so as to be confident of being the true parent of any offspring, thereby ensuring that the male's (assumed) investment is not wasted on the offspring of another male. Avoiding the 'cuckoo' problem – of being cuckolded. The trouble with this notion is legion, even when you set aside questions as to whether there actually is any investment; as I will outline over succeeding sections.

## SECTION 15

## MEN'S 'MATE-GUARDING' IS NOT WHAT IT SEEMS

The idea that men have proprietorial 'control' over women arises in biology as the concept of 'mate guarding': male 'mate-guarding' of females. The male supposedly stays close to the female to prevent her from initiating or accepting sexual advances from any other male. That's the theory. However, the evidence fails to stack up. How is it, that if the male is so assiduous in keeping his mate for himself, that for all sorts of ostensibly 'monogamous' species a high proportion of offspring are not fathered by the male of the pair, but instead have 'extra-pair paternity'? (e.g., Colombelli-Négrel et al, 2009; Lezalová-Piálková, 2010). We humans are no exception here. Estimates are all over the place, with the most usual in medical circles being

15%, but many believe this to be far too low. Even the most conservative figure is of a median worldwide ten percent (Baker & Bellis, 1995). If 'mate-guarding' is effective anywhere, you might think this would be in the very close-knit communities of still extant 'primitive' societies, but extra-pair paternity if rife here too (Scelza, 2011). Looking across species and reviewing all of the literature, in 1997, Joseph Manson concluded that whether or not there was 'mate-guarding', and regardless of how strongly or weakly it was exercised, it bore little relation to the extent of extra-pair paternity. The same is found when looking just at birds (Johnson & Burley, 1998). With 'mate-guarding' evidently so useless, the whole basis of it recently started to be questioned. In 2005, Hanna Kokko & Lesley Morrell asked: "if females regularly escape 'mate-guarding' attempts, we face an enigma: why does 'mate guarding' evolve if it is so inefficient?"

Well, is this merely 'inefficiency', or is it that 'mate-guarding' is not as it seems? Looking closer at how females in pair-bonds behave, it's apparent that their male partners don't stop them having sex with those other males the females choose. It's not their male 'other-halves' doing the gate-keeping, then, but the females themselves; who may pick through and select a 'superior' male. Yet these would be the very guys the male partner would be worried about; not the 'losers'. He knows he won't have a problem from that quarter. 'Mate-guarding' indeed cannot be what it has been assumed to be.

To understand what is going on, we have to see things from the female's perspective. Her choice will be pretty fussy, because she can be impregnated only by one male, and is then for years in limbo, as it were. Anyway, she has a long-term partner expressly for this job. The only reason she would shop around is if there were other males available who had a significantly better complement of genes than her husband's. She could have sex 'on the sly' with such a male and just return to her pair-bond partner. If she doesn't conceive, she still has her regular partner to fall back on. That this indeed is what is going on in the human case is confirmed by research revealing – well, confirming what everyone knows – that women behave in the very opposite way to men in *raising* their 'standards' when looking for 'casual' sex (Szepsenwol, Mikulincer & Birnbaum, 2013). Not just women, but females of other species behave in just this way (e.g.,

Cochas et al, 2006; Kempenaers et al, 1992). With the potential life-changing consequences of sex for the female, there would be no point in extra-pair sex with any male of a lower mate-value than that of her pair-bonded partner. And any male she so selects would have to be of a significantly higher mate-value than her pair-bonded partner to justify the real risk of him deserting her should her infidelity be discovered.

Switching to the male partner's perspective: the male would have no purpose in staying around with the female unavailable for impregnation for the entire duration of her gestating and giving birth to another male's offspring, and then breast-feeding for years (as it would have been ancestrally, just as today in extant 'primitive' societies), with the delay this causes to a resumption of oestrus cycling. His best course by far in this situation is to cut his losses and enter into a replacement pair-bond. And this is just how men usually behave in response to a wife's infidelity.

Why doesn't he try to stop his partner temporarily deserting him, and – surely – the other male from cuckolding him? The reason is evolutionary logic cemented in adaptive implicit psychology and stress physiology. To be a cuckolding male necessarily is to possess a comparatively higher mate-value than the male being cuckolded; and, therefore, he is likely to be the physically more powerful and/or more belligerent of the two, and/or to be a member of a stronger male coalition. Consequently, if the confrontation resolved to simple contest, then most likely the defending male would lose. Not that it would get to that point: the evolution of the facility to be part of a dominance hierarchy entails lower status males possessing the implicit psychology and stress physiology to avoid initiating or escalating conflict with higher- (but not with lower-) ranking males, thus likely avoiding from the outset the possibility of an escalation to a fight they most likely would not win. Better just to signal submission and have done with it than to have a scrap until injury prevents you from continuing. Yes, reluctantly you will be allowing sexual access to your partner, which is a deal-breaker regarding your relationship with her; but the alternative is the same plus physical injury – surely leading in turn to a fall in rank, which would mean a lowering of your ability to find a replacement for the pair-bond partner who has now rendered herself your ex.

So much, then, for male 'mate-guarding' to be the basis of pair-bonding. As hitherto understood, that is. As proprietorial control over the female partner, 'mate-guarding' must be something of a misnomer. It only can have a different function to that generally supposed. The most obvious alternative is to turn the whole conceptualisation on its head so that 'mate-guarding' serves not the interests of the male to avoid being cuckolded, but instead is a service to the female in preventing attempts at sexual access by males of *lower* mate-value (lower than that of her pair-bonded partner). This is not a new idea: it has already been suggested as what underpins pair-bonding across primate species (Norscia & Borgognini-Tarli, 2008). And before this, it had been recognised that 'mate-guarding' in part involved deterring unwanted suitors (Lumpkin, 1983), but as an exploitation by females of male 'mate-guarding' (as usually it has been understood), to extend its function. Simple male (over-)attentiveness is recognised to have costs for attractive females even in 'lowly' species (Partridge & Fowler, 1990; Long et al, 2009). Robin Dunbar, in his 2012 book, *The Science of Love and Betrayal,* grasped the reality regarding humans. He points out that the evidence shows that 'mate-guarding' should be envisaged in terms of a 'body-guard' ('hired gun') to assist the female in keeping at bay undesirable males.

Lower mate-value males do pose a problem for females. The problem is reciprocal: in low-quality males being sexually selected against by females, they are liable to face reproductive oblivion. They have little option but to employ riskier, long-odds approaches to try to court females. Not that this is likely to bear fruit, though. The females they approach invariably are too highly fertile to have an interest in sex with them. This doesn't mean that females need 'bodyguards' to avoid being raped. Within-community social prohibitions and punishments for infringement are so great that few if any males would ever go that far (even in the absence of evolved inhibition), and the worst of it usually would be some females allowing themselves to be cajoled into sex when at any other time in another frame of mind they might never agree to it. Even this is little problem though, because of the evolved feature of concealed ovulation – hidden oestrus. In rendering males unable to detect the short monthly window of fertility when it would be fruitful to gain sexual access to the female, a lower mate-value male can have no inkling of when best to time efforts to try for a one-off bout of sex that will result in conception. There is no scope here over time for males to evolve to implicitly desire to put in extra effort to obtain sex within the critical time slot (which would need to be spurred by an also-evolved sense of females appearing more attractive at this auspicious time). There is a way round this, however. It turns out that human ovulation/oestrus actually is not entirely hidden but subtly evident (e.g., Tarin & Gomez-Piquer, 2002). Detection is possible only up-close, though. That would mean, for the male, having to be 'in her face' regularly so as to spot the transition.

The problem for a female then would be continual, persistent attention from unwanted, low-status males, and a very much greater chance of any sex she relents to (or is partly coerced into) ending up in a pregnancy, because males in that scenario *would* be able to take advantage of the availability of subtle signs, by evolving to experience greater sexual desire upon detecting oestrus. Not only is this kind of male attention a problem in itself, but it crowds out and discourages approach by the high mate-value males to whom the female is potentially sexually receptive; and also effectively hinders the females' own initiatives to associate with such males. The overall impact of this is shown in experimental manipulation in 'simpler' species of male access and female fertility. The high-fertility females end up, effectively, no better off reproductively than low-fertility females, and, crucially, the disparity in reproduction between males correspondingly lessens, which thereby (in the words of the authors) "speed(s) the rate of accumulation of harmful mutation" – undermining the very basis of all that we're discussing here had evolved to counteract. In other words, it partly nullifies the effect of selection to drive the pivotal purging in the 'genetic filter' mechanism (Long et al, 2009).

This is where the other side of concealed ovulation / hidden oestrus comes into its own. Just as it works to usually render useless the mating attempts by unwanted males, it can spur sexual attention from the males the female actually wants to encourage. Women have evolved to be most receptive to extra-pair sex with high mate-value males when at the most fertile point in their menstrual cycle (e.g., Gangestad & Thornhill, 2008); so if at this time a female becomes proceptive (sexually initiating) and allows a male she favours to get particularly close, then the favoured male is in a position to detect the subtle cues that she is indeed in her fertile phase, to trigger in him more sexual interest. The mechanism of concealed ovulation can in this way be doubly discriminating in both *dis*couraging low mate-value males whilst *en*couraging high mate-value males. [The understanding here of the function of hidden oestrus easily trumps the usual thinking that either it helps ensure male investment or counteracts infanticide by males (for a review of which, see Thornhill & Gangestad, 2008). Neither male investment nor infanticide were ancestral for humans or for the ape species alive today that is the nearest to the extinct (proto-)ape common ancestor, the orang-utan. Concealed ovulation/oestrus and pair-bonding now look like related mechanisms that evolved far back in evolutionary time – likely before the beginning of the ape radiation (the differentiation into various species from a proto-ape common ancestor). There is a referenced discussion of all this in my paper on pair-bonding (Moxon, 2013).]

In the discouraging of lower-status males there arises a key role for men; even of the middling sort, not just higher-rankers. If a female can make good use of a male to stick close to her to make it clear that interest from the lowly masses is not welcome, then many males are in a position to exploit this need in conditionally offering the service only to those females whose mate-value (fertility) is higher than that of those females who would be willing to have 'no strings' sex with them – which, unless the males are notably high-ranking, would be pretty few, if any. Remember, too, that males can also key into the other basis of pair-bonding, already discussed, concerning sex-dichotomous mate-vale trajectory – female mate-value falling off a cliff with age.

Pair-bonding then would emerge as an evolved mutual trade-off between the sexes. Whilst the male acquires for regular sex a more fertile female than he could otherwise procure for 'casual' sex, the female obtains assistance *both* to optimise sexual access to her (by not the 'wrong' and only the 'right' sort of males, as it were), *and* effectively to project into the future her peak mate-value beyond her very early years of fertility, instead of sustaining the impact of its rapidly falling away. The combination of these two benefits substantially increases her total fertility – the sum total of her reproductive output in terms of quality and quantity, or her potential in this regard. The upshot is that pair-bonding must have evolved in the female interest, only then serving male interests on its coat-tails.

## SECTION 16

## WOMEN VALUE PAIR-BONDING MORE THAN MEN DO

It ought, then, to be apparent that women more than men value pair-bonding, and this is just what is found when research taps into implicit rather than explicit cognition – surveys of attitudes to marriage are worse than useless in that they fail to exclude and instead evoke perennial prejudices couched in contemporary political fashion. Ditto divorce statistics regarding the sex of the initiator (formal separation proceedings are likely the response to de facto separation initiated by the other partner, or to the other partner's indifferent inertia; as well as – for women – to very strong financial and child custody incentives). The trick is to key into the individual's indirect measures of concern for / interest in his/her pair-bonding status, so that he/she, in being unaware of what is being examined, cannot explicitly express a view. What comes out is relatively unglossed 'gut feeling'. Cognition that is essentially unchanged as it emerges from a non-conscious level, not subject to censorship by social inhibition. The data thereby is uncontaminated with political and other bias.

A neat window is provided by patterns of mobile phone usage. Robin Dunbar and his associates (listed as Palchykov et al, 2012) find that women invest far more heavily than men in a pair-bond, and persist with it as their principal focus on average more than fully twice as long: for fifteen years, compared to men's average of just seven – strikingly corresponding to the famed 'seven-year itch'. It's quite a lot longer than Helen Fisher's average four years, and might even indicate an adaptation for the male to stay with the female for *three* successive conceptions rather than two.

Another angle is provided by surveying the extent of worry about partner infidelity. A very large cross-cultural study revealed that wives were far more exercised in this respect than were husbands (Shattuck et al, 2012). This is startling given that the major problem for males of cuckoldry – the importation of a genetic complement to offspring from outside of the pair-bond – has no parallel for women. An objective male concern, it's long been studied in terms of the profound sex differences in what evokes jealousy: males are much more sensitive to sexual betrayal than are women, who are far more bothered by emotional disloyalty than are men, because it heralds desertion. [There is a big literature on this, and a 'meta-analytic' review (a statistical comparison across methodologically disparate studies) by Brad Sagarin et al (2012) of both real-life surveys and hypothetical scenarios in experiments confirms a real sex difference.] The sort of infidelity both sexes indulge in as extra-pair sex is just that: extra-pair *sex* rather than a fully-fledged emotional relationship. Infidelity in marriage usually is about re-finding the sexual excitement that always fades over time; not to try to substitute a new emotional tie for the one that still exists and usually has been augmented by new forms of attachment. With females objectively having far less to fear, in facing no consequences of the very sort of infidelity in which males especially usually indulge – plain promiscuous sex – then Robin Dunbar's team's (Shattuck et al's) findings would seem to be rooted in men's lack of concern for the integrity of the pair-bond. Perhaps the most robust evidence of all regarding this topic is the stuff of stereotype – the colloquial rule-of-thumb born of long-standing observation. One of the most common conversational staples is that the woman 'stands by her man' despite his infidelities, whilst the man may well desert at the first sign of his female partner's unfaithfulness.

Most tellingly, research reveals that it's not men rather than women who typically try to prevent their partner from straying by 'controlling' behaviour. It's the other way round. David Vogel and his team (2007) find overall that the woman partner has complete charge of the relationship, both taking responsibility in representing it to the world outside and acting within it in such a domineering fashion that the man is left with nowhere to go except to give in. Exactly in line with this, Diane Coleman and Murray Straus long ago (1986) found that the woman is the 'controlling' partner in 90% of couples. Women even utilise male modes of 'control' at least as much as do men (Graham-Kevan & Archer, 2009). As they will hugely if not exclusively predominate in female modes (because males wish to avoid ever being considered even remotely 'wussy', given the potential impact on their rank!), then, again, women would emerge as the 'controlling' party. Most recently, Elizabeth Bates tested the standard assumption of male control and found that "women were more likely than men to be categorized as showing high control" (Bates, Graham-Kevan & Archer, 2014). That the female ruling the roost was always the popular understanding can be seen from this having been the only theme to rival sex celebrated in rueful humour in the raunchy English postcards of old that were such a major presence at seaside resorts.

With women valuing their pair-bond much more than men, and for this to be readily apparent in various ways, and not least in 'controlling' behaviour, and with this having a profound basis – pair-bonding clearly evolved in the female interest; then it would follow that aggression within sexual partnerships would be expected to take a surprising turn. It is known that domestic violence – (intimate-) partner violence – arises out of 'controlling' behaviour; the attempts to retain the partner (e.g., Dasgupta,1999; Felson & Outlaw, 2007). Actually, then, partner violence is more likely to be *female*-perpetrated, and not at all to resemble what it is popularly supposed to be. Well, I say 'popularly supposed', but this is of course an imposition from on-high: the view of ordinary people below the surface and, until very recently, explicitly, is just as is revealed in a prime topic of those aforesaid English saucy seaside postcards since the 19th century through their long heyday beginning in the 1930s and continuing right up through the late 1970s. The hapless husband fleeing his red-faced frying-pan or rolling-pin wielding wife. This was a main plank of humour hardly through its being an exception to the rule, but because it was something with which everyone easily and ruefully could identify. It was a portrayal in a single clear image of an essential reality. The comic truth stems from what superficially might seem a dominance-subdominance (submission) topsy-turviness, but which in fact is a different kind of 'control' – that could lead to pretty serious injury given the heavy objects being wielded.

## SECTION 17

## WOMEN ARE MUCH THE MORE VIOLENT TO THEIR PARTNERS

Recent work by the prominent researchers into female aggression, Ann Campbell and Catherine Cross, has revealed that physical violence within sexual relationships is not merely one mode of aggression that women and girls may resort to, but is their *preferred* mode in this context. If the findings re women are astonishing, Campbell's team's findings regarding men are fully in line with common experience. In total contrast, men and boys back away from being physically aggressive in any situation where a female would be the target, with the context of a couple (sexual partnership) being no exception (Cross, Tee & Campbell, 2011; Cross & Campbell, 2012). This was strongly echoed, subsequently by Szell & Thurner (2013), in their finding that males hesitate to reciprocate hostile actions of females. Consequently, looking overall at violence between the sexes, women are responsible for three times as much as are men (Morse, 1995). Putting the studies together, they explain why partner violence is far higher in lesbian couples – it has been known for some time to be two to three times the rates for heterosexuals, and substantially higher than for 'gay' couples, the rates for which are intermediate between those for heterosexual and female homosexual couples, despite the seemingly ripe scenario for physical aggression of male against male (Coleman, 1990; Bologna, Waterman & Dawson, 1987; Lie et al, 1991).

Clear as is the research by Campbell's team, it has become especially neat with the subsequent discovery of both the neural circuitry responsible for the male-specific self-inhibition of violence to females and the hormonal basis of female preference for violence over other forms of aggression in a couple context. The former was the work of neuroscientists looking for crucial, evolutionarily highly conserved neural pathways as the basis of human aggression. They uncovered a three-tier neural pathway (all of which is found only in males) thought to be common across species to include humans, serving to nearly eliminate aggression, triggered by close physical contact of any kind with a female (Yuan et al, 2014). This neural pathway does not make use of any other learning and memory circuitry, appearing to have evolved as a standalone mechanism just for this function, indicating that it's a crucial adaptation. Its usefulness is pretty self-apparent: obviating the risk of any impact on a female sexual partner of aggression by displacement from common and serious male-male violence. In other words, it stops a husband who's had a very bad day and then drowned his sorrows from inadvertently catching the wife in venting his frustration, or actually targeting her if he 'loses it' more completely and indiscriminately lashes out at or focuses upon whomever happens to be there (at home, this usually being the wife, of course).

The hormonal basis of female preference for violence over other forms of aggression in a couple context has been revealed to be oxytocin: the very hormone underpinning pair-bonding. It prompts women (though not, or much less so, men) to perpetrate partner violence, notwithstanding that the effect depends on a degree of general aggressiveness (which in other scenarios is more a quality of males than of females) (DeWall et al, 2014). As DeWall points out (and others had found) although oxytocin does prompt violence in males, it's against a different kind of target: 'out-group' members – stranger males. The link between oxytocin and partner violence is particularly revealing in that in other species oxytocin underpins maternal aggression (fierce defence of the female's own young), which, in being the evolutionarily-ancient key form of female violence, appears to be homologous (having a shared evolutionary origin and equivalent if seemingly different function) to partner violence. Supporting this conclusion is the completely different neuro-hormonal basis of maternal aggression from that of within-sex aggression (Gammie et al, 2008); and that it is fearless, just as is female-perpetrated partner violence (in being actively preferred over employing other modes of aggression, even though the male target has huge potential to respond with far greater hitting power, and against the far weaker female body frame and facial bone structure). Evolutionary theorists already had put oxytocin in the frame regarding 'mate-retention' behaviour; and maternal aggression in defence of offspring would seem not far removed functionally from female aggression in defence of the means of producing offspring (the male partner). Its co-option in the evolutionary process would be a simple, minor instance of this common sort of development.

With no male equivalent of maternal aggression, then all this strongly suggests that there is no male-equivalent aetiology (set of causes) regarding partner violence perpetration. In other words, as regards the opposite sex, men appear not to be physically aggressive per se. [Note that this of course does not mean that there is no male perpetration, but that it is likely not partner violence per se. Either the aggression is not with intent or it's not directed as such at the female target but instead is by displacement – presumably, often alcohol-fuelled. Exceptions would be psychopathic violence (which is non-discriminating: it's against anybody) and that by otherwise psychologically abnormal males, which indeed *is* partner violence per se, but not by 'normal' males.]

The foregoing research into the particular nature and neuro-hormonal basis of partner violence is just one line of evidence among several that all converge on the complete inversion of the usual rhetoric. Another is that the huge sex differentials in upper-body strength and body-frame weakness are not at all reflected in partner violence injury rates: the combination of much superior male hitting power and far greater female susceptibility to injury, the forensic psychologist Louise Dixon calculates should produce a twenty-fold excess of injuries in women. That's even on the assumption of equal rates of perpetration by men towards women and women towards men, never mind if men were the more violent. In other words, at the very least, 95% of all partner violence injuries would be expected to be sustained by women, and just 5% by men (Dixon, 2012). Not a bit of it. The actual sex ratio in injury rates is not only not even remotely on this huge scale, but there is no skew towards women at all; and, still more, where it most counts, the sex ratio is actually *reversed* and not insubstantially so: regarding by far the most important category, serious injury, victims are very much more likely to be male (Felson & Cares, 2005). For injuries overall, it's roughly parity if you admit of a balancing of the excess of serious injuries sustained by men with a small excess of females sustaining minor injuries; which, of course, for both sexes are far more common and far less significant. Researchers are in broad agreement. Injuries as a whole are either slightly higher for women (Archer, 2000; Mirrlees-Black et al, 1998), or the sex difference is not significant (Capaldi & Owen, 2001), or nil (George, 2003). The only sense that can be made of this vast disparity between the expected and actual data is that it indirectly reveals a very large preponderance of female perpetration of partner violence over that by males.

How this has been hidden is no secret. Partner violence data is very well understood to suffer from a highly sex-differential reporting bias, with men not just far, far less willing to report to police than are women, but unwilling also to report to researchers. Making a complaint to police is a big deal; not so filling in a survey, re which you don't even need to supply your name: they're anonymous by design. So this isn't merely an issue of the obvious social stigma but of deep-seated psychology. Men, unlike women, do not readily self-perceive victimhood, even with the aggressor being another man – it would be an explicit admission of a fall in status and consequently a gateway to a further fall in status; anathema to the male. When it comes to being a victim of a female aggressor, male denial of being a victim is likely to be still more profound, in that physically aggressive contest across sex is meaningless. As we have seen, men and women never engage with each other in dominance-submission terms. Men will signal deference to women. Neither do men engage with women in terms of the standard notion of 'mate-guarding': as I have outlined, male 'mate-guarding' as hitherto conceived is a fiction. So, with no (or, at least, a lack of a) male behavioural counterpart of female 'controlling' behaviour, then this manifested as partner violence is likely to nonplus males. The sex differential in reporting has been measured by leading US investigators of partner violence, Jan Stets and Murray Straus, to be by as much as a factor of ten (Stets & Straus, 1990). Even the UK Office of National Statistics (ONS), in the UK 2012/13 Crime Survey, concedes that it's by a factor of three (ONS,

2014), but then fails to make any adjustment to its data to even begin to take this into account. Couching surveys in terms of crime or personal safety always evokes a victim response in women and the very opposite in men; but even after making major efforts to remove such 'demand characteristics', John Archer (the leading UK expert in aggression research, with a particular interest in partner violence), found that men still considerably under-report compared to women (Archer, 1999).

The great bulk of partner violence data has not been produced by such stringent filtering, and therefore massively under-states the proportion of male victims, and in consequence indirectly vastly *over*-states the proportion of victims who are female – and, therefore, vastly under-states the proportion of perpetrators who are female. Despite this, the proportion of male victims as recorded in the UK official crime survey is consistently 40% (e.g., Thompson, 2010); a far higher proportion than most people realise, because although it is not infrequently reported in the media, it's couched within the framework of the ubiquitous extreme-feminist perspective. It tends to get lost 'in plain sight', as it were. The point is that if even the most conservative measure or estimate of the sex-differential in the propensity to report were factored into the official crime data – and, to reiterate, formal reporting by men either of a crime and/or to police will be much less even than their low rate of their reporting in anonymous survey – then there would be revealed an overwhelming preponderance of male victims, completely reversing what is the mistaken current public perception of partner violence perpetration and victimhood. When you move away from crime stats and crime surveys to the academic research proper, then the proportion of female perpetration increases from 40% to what researchers even conservatively in their conclusions reveal with expressions such as 'at least as much as' or 'similar if not greater than' or 'as much or more than' male (e.g., Fiebert, 2014; Archer, 2000; Dutton, 2012). The female is at least twice as likely to initiate partner violence, whether her partner responds in kind (Whitaker et al, 2007) or doesn't (Williams et al, 2001; Anderson, 2002; Ehrensaft & Vivian, 1999); and as the violence gets more serious, this sex differential rises to threefold (Stets & Straus, 1990) or sixfold (Magdol et al, 1997). Looking at all studies examining one-way partner violence, bar those re police reports it is always more by women, regardless of how sampling is done (Langhinrichsen-Rohling, Selwyn & Rohling, 2012) – police reports make for worse than useless data, for the reasons above-discussed. Overall, pooled prevalence of rates of female perpetration are significantly greater than that by males (Desmarais et al, 2012b), irrespective of the type of sample or study.

## Section 18

## In 'Traditional' Societies, Women Vie to 'Honestly Signal' Fidelity

Another window on the pair-bond as being much more central for the female is how far women will go in trying to acquire a pair-bond partner by 'honestly signalling' the unlikelihood of (or intention not to engage in) their future infidelity. This can be by a variety of what otherwise appear bizarre, extreme, disparate cultural practices, that mistakenly have been taken to be imposed on women by men. Most commonly, in an array of different cultures, there is face veiling / body covering or female genital mutilation ('female circumcision') (FGM). As an example of a practice that is more culture-specific and localised, there is Chinese foot-binding. All are conspicuously effective to a marked degree at physically taking women out of the extra-pair sex market, as it were. All are practices occurring firmly within female sociality, well away from males. All originated with the most privileged women (noblewomen), only later disseminating down to women in the lower social orders. These are findings and conclusions that will be a great surprise to most, and as also this is a topic on which I'm not previously published, then I'll now provide a mini review, focusing on the most well researched of these phenomena – FGM – before going on to more briefly show that the others are similar.

Though seemingly the most unfathomable of these customs, FGM in a way is the most familiar through the far more common (to us in the West) corresponding male GM above-discussed. Just as partial foreskin removal denudes sexual sensitivity and, thereby, inclination towards sex, FGM likewise is the physical denuding of sexual response. That sexual sensitivity and predilection to 'casual' sex indeed is curtailed is both the experience and the belief of women in 'traditional' societies where FGM is still ubiquitous. Fran Hosken discovered that half of all 'cut' women say they do not enjoy sex at all, and that it would be impossible for women to control their own sexuality and remain faithful to their husbands without 'cutting' to reduce sexual sensitivity (Hosken, 1983; 1989). Mary Lindner (2008) similarly finds that both young women and their relatives believe FGM curbs sexual desire, 'purifying' the girl into a 'treasure' to make a chaste wife for an eligible man. According to Elin Sæverås (2003), male partners complain that sex is far less enjoyable with 'cut' women because they are at best passive, if not actually suffering. The denuding of sexual response is confirmed by research. Ike Onyishi and team have published just this year that, in a traditional African society, women who have been subject to 'cutting' are much less likely to have "uncommitted sex" – extra-pair sex, in other words – for the reason that they lack the necessary desire, attitude and styles of behaviour.

Here the equivalence of FGM and MGM ends though, because there is no corresponding 'policing' of females. 'Policing' of males is in the interests of females even more than of males, but far from any sort of 'policing' of *females* being in the interests of males, men would much prefer women to have *enhanced* desire for extra-pair sex, not its denuding. In particular, it would be welcomed by high-mate-value males, because a female greater willingness to engage in extra-pair sex is of actual benefit mostly to such males; these being the sort of males of interest to females as extra-pair sex partners. Yet these are the very men 'in charge', as it were; that feminist 'theory' would deem responsible for imposing the practice, if indeed this was the basis of FGM. The usual assumption is a non-starter, then. Any 'policing' of females here would make sense only as being *by* females. FGM must be female within-sex competition.

How, though, could a lessened availability of extra-pair sex be of benefit to females? It might be thought that it could serve to keep pair-bonds intact by restricting the availability of the alternative, but men don't desert their female pair-bond partners in favour of extra-pair sex.

It's called 'extra-pair' for good reason. Neither would the value of pair-bonding be bolstered, because not only is extra-pair sex anyway pretty well unavailable to most males, but it's a safety valve against the male partner's temptation to seek a replacement pair-bond as his female partner's attractiveness quickly fades with age. If neither of these possibilities could significantly up the ante re pair-bonding, then what can?

The way that a denuded sexual response really would be in the service of women's within-sex competition is if it were to signal a readiness to be faithful to a prospective pair-bond partner. This would most count where the male is very high status, because it's for the likes of him that female-female competition would be fiercest; and such a male would be especially fearful of an unfaithful wife, given that the other men in his rarefied social circle are just the sort with whom women are likely to be unfaithful. It would be expected, then, that FGM would originate with and be restricted to noble-women, only gradually to disseminate down to those more ordinary as more and more women were obliged to follow suit if they were to have any chance of 'marrying up'.

We cannot know one way or the other if this is what happened in 'traditional' societies, because with no culture of writing they have no historical record; but given its currency in ancient 'civilisations' its origin must pre-date even the very earliest historical record. It was current even when Herodotus was writing in 500BC. Kathy Naddesen (2000) summarises that: "In ancient times FGM had a definite class component as it was performed only on women from the upper socio-economic echelons and on relatives of priests and rulers".

That FGM is a female within-sex phenomenon is abundantly apparent in only women being practitioners (except where, in attempting to minimise harm, contemporarily it has become medicalised, or, in a few places, sometimes the village barber is employed). Usually it's the mother, grandmother or local specialist 'cutter'; generally an elderly woman of the community (Lindner, 2008). Sæverås found that "a grandmother may set up the circumcision of her granddaughter even if the child's mother is against it. Friends may do the 'operation' on the daughter while the mother is away". The mother-in-law is also regularly cited, though it seems that rather than relatives the bulk of operations are done by the older female 'specialist' (Worku Zerai / Norwegian Church Aid, 2003). Sæverås points to the power of the 'exciser': in being often also the community birth attender and/or healer, she's held in great respect. JM Koroma (2002) summarises: "FGM is women's business and they more actively perpetuate FGM than do men. ... decision-making for undergoing the operation is in large part made by mothers, although there are instances where it is a joint decision by both mother and father with the latter 'only informed to obtain his blessings'. Other decision-makers are other female family members, particularly grandparents". Richard Shweder (2000) writes that: "the practice is almost always controlled, performed, and most strongly upheld by women, ... men have rather little to do with these female operations, may not know very much about them, and may feel it is not really their business to interfere or to try to tell their wives, mothers, aunts, and grandmothers what to do. It is the women of the society who are the cultural experts in this intimate feminine domain, and they are not particularly inclined to give up their powers or share their secrets". Agnetha Hejll observes (2001) that "all too often men see FGM as 'women's business'. This is understandable in societies that segregate the sexes and where men and women seldom discuss sexuality. Women also keep men out of the matter".

It is not merely that women perform FGM, then, but that they make the *decision* that FGM should be carried out, and they also exclude men. Tellingly, it is not the men but the women themselves who *support* FGM. Shetty Priya (2007) concludes "it is much more difficult to convince the women to give it up, than to convince the men". The anthropologist Nelly Ali complains (2012) of "the cultural resistance of women, more than men" to rejecting FGM. Simon Rye (2002) finds that "many many men find it a problematic part of their culture". In a 2007 UNFPA report, it's stated that "paradoxically it is Maasai women, more than men, who have insisted on keeping the tradition of FGM/C alive ... most men, once they understand what the practice entails, are horrified by it and oppose it ... in their extra-marital relations they prefer uncircumcised women from other communities". Formal surveys have been conducted across several countries, confirming that smaller proportions of men than women support FGM (Population Council, 1999; Population Reference Bureau, 2001). Even in countries where concerted campaigning to dissuade women has already led to a major shift away from supporting FGM, it's still not amongst women that opposition is strongest. Women lag behind men in this regard. Mary Lindner, in her own survey, finds 79% of all male participants do not support FGM, which is significantly more than the 67% of women.

All the signs, then, are that far from FGM being imposed on women by men, it is a practice that is perpetuated by women, just as it was started by them – and by noble-women, at that. The same is the case for face/body 'veiling'. As with FGM, the custom is ancient, pre-dating the Islamic religion by thousands of years, and occurring across a number of empires. In Mesopotamia and Persia, veiling was restricted to elite, married, free women, and was actively forbidden to poor and single women, prostitutes and slaves (Nielson, 2009). So keen were women more generally to adopt the veil that punishments had to be devised to stop them doing so. In Assyria, veiled servants and prostitutes could have their garments confiscated, be given fifty blows and tar poured over them (Kinias, 2010). So unconcerned were men with the practice that, far from upholding it, they had to be faced with serious punishments for failing to report inappropriate veiling: imprisonment, mutilation or public flogging (Nemet-Nejat, 1998).

Just as for veiling and FGM, so also for Chinese foot-binding, which, as a drastic progressive mis-shaping of the feet through wrapping them extremely tightly in wet material that contracts as it dries out, all too concretely meant that a woman was physically hidebound from straying too far from her future marital home, albeit that it allowed more mobility than many have supposed. The assumed purpose of creating dainty feet was a latter-day rationalisation. This much and more can be gleaned from the detailed accounts, of which there is no shortage; notably the full texts of the works cited below on specific points. Foot-binding is taken to be of relatively recent origin (a millennium, though it might be far far older), belonging to the civilisation having the oldest written record, and, therefore, with a clearer history of dissemination, albeit that the precise origin remains cloudy. Gerry Mackie (1996) writes that "it spread from the Imperial palace, to court circles, to the larger upper classes, and then to the middle and lower classes". Women were always the practitioners and 'in charge'. Dorothy Ko (2008) points out that women bound their *own* and their daughters' feet. The 'matriarchy' from both families of a couple were behind foot-binding: marriage selection requiring foot-bound discipline was the responsibility of the prospective mother-in-law, according to C Fred Blake (1994). Wang Ping (2000) tellingly relates that the practice "produced permanent bonding with (their) mother(s) and female ancestors". So taken with it were women that through the ages repeated attempts at banning by emperors failed and were reversed (Levy, 1992), and after the Nationalists also failed in the mid-twentieth century, it took draconian repression by the Communists finally to stop it.

Pooling all of the accounts, it's clear that acquiring a pair-bond partner – necessarily competing with other women in this regard – was the root of the custom. There was the usual fear of not being able to find a husband and the equally usual outcasting as lewd, should the practice be omitted; give-aways here, just as re FGM and veiling. And here, again, we see that mothers, family 'matriarchs', female village elders and 'professional' specialist practitioners were behind and to the fore regarding all aspects of the custom – introducing girls to it, carrying out the procedures and monitoring that it's adhered to.

I discovered that there is a prior review that likewise pulled together the seemingly disparate phenomena of FGM, veiling and foot-binding, and it also took an evolutionary perspective: that by psychology Professor Roy Baumeister. In his long 2002 paper, *Cultural Suppression of Female Sexuality*, he finds that the common strand is within-sex competitiveness, in line with my own general conclusion about these practises. Their range may be further extended: back in 1988, Riadh Abed had concluded that the female cult for thinness and resultant eating disorders should be considered in just these terms.

So do men fit into these customs beyond being just the subject of women's within-sex competition? How is it that they have been mistaken for key agents? Well, certainly, women may beseech men to use their civic role to espouse on their behalf the need to continue the practices. With the male sense of in-group mapping perfectly on to the whole community, having evolved to function to provide whole-community defence; then men will feel an onus on them to do women's bidding. In respect of ubiquitous ingrained culture, notwithstanding its being entirely within the female domain, it should be expected that males in their civic duty would feel obliged to support females if there were any risk of lax adherence by some women to their within-sex custom. Given evolved 'policing' of males driving a natural default prejudice, in effect to blame males for their own 'policing', then it can easily be seen how we can make the mistake of supposing that men 'control' women's sexuality when in fact it is a case of 'sisters doing it to themselves', as it were. Of course, feminist ideologues would invert reality and claim that women are obliged to do as they do in anticipation of the 'male power' held in reserve against them should they not do so; but this is the usual unfalsifiability of a (thereby non-)theory unable to show its actual colours for fear of the evidence that would pile up against it. The nature of within-sex competitiveness of one sex cannot be 'blamed' on the other. Pair-bonding evolved in the female interest, to be an imposition on the male. Males hardly, then, can be held responsible for how women try to further leverage what is in women's own interests.

## SECTION 19

## THE FEMALE WITHIN THE MALE SOCIAL STRUCTURE

Moving away now from pair-bonding and its ramifications, to return to more general sociality: where things get really interesting is when we move beyond how the sexes think and behave across sex one-on-one, to how they do so group-on-group – to how, *then*, they behave both within- and cross-sexually. Here we can expect several principles outlined above to come together. In 2009, Priya Raghubir & Ana Valenzuela had the inspired idea of analysing what goes on between and within the sexes in *The Weakest Link* TV quiz programme. On the assumption that all readers (on both sides of the pond) are familiar with this ultimate of all game shows, these studies reveal, quite beautifully, the female within-sex dynamics of, on the one hand, same-sex preference, and, on the other, same-sex exclusion; and actual male deference towards females. Men don't exclude a woman in what is here a co-operative cum competitive contest scenario, unless the woman is performing particularly badly *and* there is no man who is poorly performing. Males will get rid of male poor performers first. This is clear male deference to females. By contrast, women will exclude either men or fellow women *despite their good performance* – respectively, through female same-sex 'in-grouping' bias and (what the authors dub 'queen bee') same-sex derogation. The authors don't attempt to unravel 'same-sex derogation'. Is the disdain a female has for other females here through them not being in her 'personal network'?

The male 'whole-group' co-operative behaviour holds through the early rounds, where the men readily see that it serves to accumulate prize money; only in the later rounds may they seemingly act individually to remove a threat to themselves to try to go on to win the prize total. However, this too is likely not what it seems; instead being an indirect consequence of men retaining even poorly performing women. The upshot is that males see the whole group as their co-operative group, irrespective of the sex of its members, whereas females see only other females as being potentially their in-group cohorts (hence excluding men); but with women *non*-co-operative in being exclusionary from the outset, then not only is there no 'personal networking' established – how could there be in such short time of meeting? – but it may well be that females are expressing resentment at the sex-inappropriateness of high performance in a male type of competitive scenario.

What is found in *The Weakest Link* is also discoverable in formal experimental settings to test within- versus between-sex behaviour. As Abraham Buunk and Karlijn Massar (2012) anticipated, men were more competitive in their behaviour towards another man than towards a woman, and behaved more pro-socially towards women. Women were very different, in that they were not reciprocally pro-social towards men, and in terms of ostensible competitiveness did not seem to distinguish between men and women. Looking beyond just comparing and contrasting within- and between-sex behaviour to the nature of associated brain activity, and how this is or is not synchronised across individuals, Joseph Baker et al (2016) found that both in same- or cross-sex combination, men acted co-operatively; women much less so. The males together were the most co-operative, followed by males and females together, with all-females bringing up the rear. All of the co-operativeness above the female-female baseline was through male, not any female effort – the males make all the effort in male-female groupings. There was inter-brain coherence for same-sex but not cross-sex combinations. The only combination where there appeared to be attempts by either party to understand the other's intentions and motives were males in same-sex combination. All in all, the Baker studies are a particularly illuminating window on sociality that deserves to be the start of a new research programme into the more interesting complexities of permutations of sex and grouping.

Moving from experiment or contrived scenario to the real world: there is nowhere better to go looking for a sexual conundrum to solve than the cauldron that is the contemporary workplace. What sets this up is that the world of work doesn't run efficiently or profitably unless organised hierarchically and all-inclusively: it's necessarily structured akin to male sociality. It's at the civic, all-inclusive pole of sociality, and not at the nepotistic, exclusionary opposite end of life. Management is a (prestige rather than dominance) ranking system, and each department and the organisation as a whole are readily seen by males as all-inclusive symbolic groupings: they correspond to a male sense of 'in-grouping'. Men, will, therefore, feel at home and have an arena conducive to competing with other men for meaningful position (rank), as they are motivated at their core in order to gain the status required to be chosen by women. A problem would be expected to arise for men if the proportion of women in the workplace rises to become predominant, because not only does the relative lack of men reduce their scope for mutual competitiveness, but men's competitiveness surely would be dampened through the deference that the presence of so many women would evoke.

So how, then, in comparison, do females fit in down the office? Not very well in some important ways, though in other ways they fit in neatly – and they do very well indeed in their being able to see, up-close, high-status males they may then choose to sexually select. In contrast to the male form of sociality that structures every workplace, 'female personal networking' is, as I outlined above, small-scale, hierarchically flat, exclusionary, and, in its chaining, is more likely to cut across than to be in sync with the formal way that the workplace is both divided and integrated. Exactly this was found by Adam Kleinbaum, Toby Stuart & Michael Tushman in their 2011 study of formal organisations: "women communicate differently: relative to male-male and male-female pairings, female-female interactions are much more likely to occur across organizational boundaries". Female workers will tend, then, not to identify well, either with their department or with the whole organisation, and neither with their own place in the company's formal 'pecking order'. Female managers will tend to construct their own idiosyncratic personalised, exclusionary social existence at odds with both hierarchy and sense of grouping, ignoring in particular males, but also most other females. Women toiling under a female boss may be lucky enough to be within her manager's 'personal network', but more usually will be outside of it, and made to feel excluded, with any tickings-off highly personalised and on both sides never forgotten. The larger the workplace and the divisions within it, then the worse this problem is bound to be, given the highly restricted size of female intimate grouping not growing commensurate with the increasing size of the surrounding male-style socially inclusive mass. To make matters worse, enmity is liable to be reciprocal. Female underlings are likely to view their same-sex bosses as incongruously situated within a male sociality, so that questions arise – even if they are implicit rather than explicit – about the woman manager positioning herself to gain advantage in the mating game. In this regard, the female boss is almost bound to come across as playing a double game of using feminine wiles at the same time as aping men, so as to gain 'unfair' advantage. All of this combines to make women wish for even an incompetent male boss to replace their female one – exactly the stated desire of some women when surveyed.

Women's aversion to a woman as their line manager is the most marked, consistent feature of all research of the workplace. *Gallup* continually polls on this question and has done so since 1953, and throughout the whole period it has always been the case that more women have indicated they prefer a male rather than a female boss; and every time by a greater margin even than men feel (Riffkin, 2014) – this being surprising given the fourfold same-sex 'in-grouping' bias of women translating into men being much more excluded by a female boss even than are other women. These findings are regularly reproduced whether by extensive but non-scientific survey (e.g., the Alfred Marks Agency, the Royal Mail, Harper's Bazaar) or more formally and rigorously (Molm, 1986; Mavin & Bryans, 2003; Mavin & Lockwood, 2004). Some studies invoke an ideological assumed explanation in terms of 'misogyny' (*sic*) fancifully convoluted into 'internalised misogyny' (*sic*), as mentioned above re 'policing'; an interpretation deserving short shrift.

What actually is going on in women disliking having a female manager is revealed in the answers women give when probed; the most common being that the female manager treats them unfairly, personalises everything, and bears grudges – none of which behaviour they normally experience from male managers, they claim. This rather black-and-white female/male distinction seems to be too rosy a view of male managers, smacking of disdain between female managers and their staffers travelling upwards as well as downwards: more than just reaction by the female underlings to how their female boss treats them. In 2011, Crystal Hoyt & Stefanie Simon investigated whether female leaders are at all inspiring role models for women rather than actually injurious, and conclude the latter: "upward social comparisons to high-level female leaders will have a relatively detrimental impact on women's self-perceptions and leadership aspirations". Looking up at male leaders, by contrast, has no such negative impact. Women don't like themselves in looking 'up' at their woman manager, as if they fear what they would become if they were in their boss' shoes. 'As if'? It seems to be exactly what they fear: apparently, losing their femininity.

All of these responses are very much in line with female sociality being decidedly at odds with the structure of the workplace, given that the latter necessarily is in line with male sociality. Alternative explanation is not only ideological rather than scientific, but is transparently hopeful rather than plausible.

# SECTION 20

## WOMEN RISE BY BEING MORE CONSCIENTIOUS

Notwithstanding, though, that women intrinsically are mismatched to the workplace in the nature of their sociality, women *do* fit into the workplace, and not just through choosing female-sex-typical work sectors and/or niches – which women do in large measure. In comparison to men, women are more conscientiousness (e.g., Kling, Noftle & Robins, 2013); this being an important if not the most important quality linked to success in the workplace. However, the literature is confusing, with indications that what may be considered sub-traits of conscientiousness may be key; notably the male strengths of achievement-striving and independence, or (what may be thought the more female attributes) of diligence / self-discipline. In other words, conscientiousness should be considered an aggregation of traits that as such is not at a sufficiently fine resolution to usefully examine sex difference, whereas examining constituent traits reveals them to polarise into male and female strengths. I'm not citing studies because they may be misleading in often being in respect of higher education, which is taken as proxy for the workplace when there may be no correspondence or even an inverse relationship in some aspects; and, in any case, data suffers from the big problem that the sexes usually are pooled, thereby either hiding an effect or passing it off as general when it could apply to one sex mainly or only. Indeed, it may be that a global trait of conscientiousness is less predictive of success for men than for women, or for men only in particular contexts: it is found to be associated with status in the context of individual, technical work, but not where team-work is involved (Anderson, Spataro & Flynn, 2008). Another issue is that workplace achievement may be taken to be the ability to obtain and maintain employment, when this can be for easy-to-obtain work retained through lack of an ability to secure better alternatives: a world away from what is required for career progression. As is standard in social research, investigation is bedevilled by assumptions that even when explicit are not treated as the variables they are. [This topic is complex, requiring a review for a proper discussion, but that would be tangential to the present exposition.]

With the female evolved concern for and ability regarding childcare and establishing & maintaining the 'nest', as it were; then it is no surprise that greater female than male conscientiousness is a researched finding. This is quite different to men's facility to focus on the task at hand (Moir & Moir, 1998), which is through male neural processing power over connectivity. [The male brain is much more modular than the female, and has considerably less connection between the two hemispheres, as well as increased structural connectivity related to sub-networks of executive function, as opposed, in women, to those of social motivation (Tunç et al, 2016).] Still, conscientiousness is no less of a key quality of use in the workplace – particularly in respect of low-level positions, where pay is no motivation and employers usually have to rely on staff showing a natural goodwill and work ethic. Being conscientious can, then, effectively trap an employee in an entry-level job; though it is also a quality facilitating promotion out of it. The problem is that in the absence of the competitive imperative so core to men, and the corollary of the male facility to intensely focus on a task; then few women are likely even to *want* to join men in the upper echelons of the workplace (or of any other sort of) organisation. In 2016, Sun Young Lee, Selin Kesebir & Madan Pillutla looked at female-female competition within the workplace, and they "predicted and found in one correlational study and three experiments that women regard competition with their same-gender co-workers as less desirable than men do, and that their relationships with each other suffer in the presence of competition", concluding that competition is at odds with the norm of female relationships.

Women tend to rise only so far as middling staffers, and many of these have done so in part by opting for the aforesaid female sex-typical niches, such as human resources, just as they often opt for female-friendly work sectors like healthcare and teaching. Part-time working (and, for many women, not working at all) is preferred, irrespective of having or intending a family, and only if there are good working conditions and a conducive social aspect (Hakim, 2004, 2003, 2000), regarding which most women aim for 'satisficing' (Corby & Stanworth, 2009) – not 'the best' but any job, regardless of intrinsic value or prospects, as long as it meets their range of minimum requirements. [It's rather odd that the 'pay gap' (*sic*) is so small, given the myriad reasons why it exists.]

Why would women make the required effort to try to gain executive positions when there is no evolved purpose served in doing so? Status does not confer mate-value on women as it does on men. Women intuitively grasp that the time required to ascend the corporate ladder will serve only to consume their prime reproductive years, at the end of which they will be very much less fertile, and correspondingly will have fallen considerably in mate-value, to become insufficiently attractive to the very male high-flyers whose paths, in their 'climbing the greasy pole', they had sought to cross. Women know implicitly that they are well placed to attract such men simply by 'being around', irrespective of their own career track or position. A conspicuous social front-end role, such as reception, is ideal. This is why competition truly enters into female sociality, and ruthlessly so, when in the offing is formal placement physically in the public eye, by winning such as singing competitions, passing acting auditions, edging out female rivals to be a TV news correspondent, etc. Visual eminence *is* desired by women when they can best flaunt themselves in terms of their bodily and facial appearance.

Exceptions will abound, needless to say, and women high-flyers could arise for a variety of reasons; but, as always with exceptions, they are considered thus because they are but the shadow of 'the rule'. The reality is that no efforts at 'social engineering' will ever bring about any sort of 'equality of outcome' where women and men are in similar proportion 'at the top', unless 'equality of opportunity' is jettisoned completely and blatant pro-female / anti-male discrimination installed in its place, paying no heed to the impact of over-promoting from a much smaller pool of what anyway in some respects would be lesser talent. Where there are apparent 'advances', they are illusory. So it is that company board membership in the UK has become more female only by the politically driven nominal appointment of women not as executives but non-executive directors. [As a result of a target recommended by the Davies Report, 2011, for 25% of all board members to be female by 2015; between March and August 2012, 55% of new FTSE100 company directors were women (up from 13% in 2010 and 30% in

2011), but every one was non-executive. All of the 18 new executive directors over the same period were men.] Those who have actually worked their way up through the business to know how to take it forward to out-compete rival companies, and in consequence were put on the board as the decision-makers having earned it ….. these are nearly all men. There are indeed some women CEOs, but such figures are few and usually marooned in a sea of men. As is loudly complained of, they rarely bring up other women with them – conspicuously failing to do so. They are said to 'pull the ladder up behind them'. So they seem not to be equivalent to the 'queen bee' presiding over the 'top clique', who, despite the exclusionary dynamic of female sociality, at least needs the validation of her 'wannabes'. Female sociality in any case is largely not hierarchical: the 'top clique' is more separate from than ranking over the rest of femininity, and is itself less a ranking pyramid than just the 'queen' being 'first among equals', as it were; with just one of her 'subjects' awaiting in the wings her fall from grace. Women high-flyers are more the 'surrogate man', which often is how they see themselves. This seems to apply well to that rare figure, the pre-eminent female genuine artist: Joni Mitchell, who many would argue is *the* greatest singer-songwriter; being a self-avowed case in point. [Note the qualification *genuine*: far more common, I would argue, is the female more posing as an artist so as to put her feminine physicality on wide public view.]

The irony is that high-flying women typically ape men and become (or were anyway) unlike the great majority of women. Worse – it has been pointedly claimed (notably by the female author of what many women consider the most insightful book ever written about women, *Knowing Woman: A Feminine Psychology*) – they appear to embody the negative sides of both sexes. Irene Clairmont de Castillejo (1973) singles out an extreme ruthlessness she considers a masculine side a woman can draw on, but that this is without the male quality of flexibility and is driven by female nepotism. This sounds like the 'queen bee'. As making a list will quickly reveal, throughout history female national leaders usually have not been less but actually *more* war-mongering and despotic to their own citizens than have been their male counterparts. Furthermore, it's often less the male rulers than their wives who have been the real authors of their violent and other excess (as another quick list also readily would reveal – to which now can be added Sarah Vine, the wife of Michael Gove, one of the contenders for the UK 2016 Conservative Party's particularly back-stabbing battle for the leadership and parliamentary premiership, who politically assassinated hitherto the shoe-in for Prime Minister, Boris Johnson). De Castillejo's analysis in *Knowing Woman* may be too harsh, in that some women high-flyers are perhaps benignly in a sense sexless, where the male-aping has reined in their femininity rather than conspired to bring out the negative aspects of it. They may have simply capitalised on the afore-cited female greater conscientiousness in pushing it to its furthest extent. The new UK prime minister, Theresa May, seems to fit this profile (though the falseness and pomposity – eclipsing even Margaret Thatcher in these respects – and absence of personality may hide one of de Castillejo's worst-of-both-sides demons). My point is that it is a chimera to imagine that putting women in high places somehow makes high places more female. 'High place' – that is, the apex of hierarchy – exists as part of and the product of male sociality and psychology (ultimately, of male biology, of course), and hardly can make any sense in other terms. That occasionally reaching the pinnacle is a man-aping or over-conscientious woman, or a ruthless 'queen bee', hardly changes this. If to be found up there in good number were women who were like the great majority of other women, albeit larger-than-life (in the way that male leaders are like other men, just writ large), then we might have to think again; but there is little if any sign.

## Section 21

## Men Really are More Competitive; Women Back Away

With its importance in underpinning the sex-dichotomy we see in the workplace, being that it *is* so conspicuously sex differential, I now ought to focus on competitiveness per se. From the whole of the foregoing account it should be apparent that males are bound to be highly competitive; that competitiveness is a quintessentially male trait, and male-male, not male-female; with competition amongst women or girls being of a very different sort and much more restrictive in nature. [Note that nobody suggests that women and girls are not competitive at all. The afore-mentioned *Mean Girls* scenario of life around the 'queen bee' gives the lie to that. The truth is that female competitiveness is highly circumscribed.] That's the theory, and, as we've seen, there is lots of evidence that the theory is right. Even so, experimental research where parameters can be controlled so as to fully investigate competitiveness is needed to see it in all its ramifications and to confirm that there is no 'fly in the ointment' theory-wise.

The most comprehensive testing to date of putative component factors or facets of sex-differentiality in competitiveness is last year (2015) by Christopher Cotten, Frank McIntyre & Joseph Price. They rule out male over-confidence and/or female under-confidence, misperceptions about male or female ability, and sex-differential preferences, and confirm that males are competitive in comparison to females because they enjoy competition or give a higher intrinsic value to winning, can better cope with the pressure of competition, and are less concerned with the possibility of any negative aspects of competition. That's a cluster of proxies for competitiveness. Clearly, males are much more competitive than are females because they are inherently far more competitive. The sex-differential really is, then, in competitiveness per se. This seems to be borne out in findings in connection with research into stress mechanism: in competition scenarios, what is salient for females is just the task itself, whereas for males it is the opponent (Bateup et al, 2002); and where for males the challenge is to achieve, females are preoccupied with the risk of failure (Stroud, Salovey & Epel, 2002).

Major new reviews of the whole body of research on the sex difference in competitiveness have been carried out by 'behavioural economists', and they end in very firm conclusions that it's not only that men are more competitive than women, but that the sexes move in diametrically opposite directions. Muriel Niederle, in her 2015 review, found overall that whereas men favour competition, women actually back away from it. Confirming this, in a particularly exhaustive consideration of all conceivable alternative explanations, Robert Deaner and team (2015) showed that this sex dichotomy persists even in highly selective sub-populations – elites, such as in athletics – where there would be expected to be female exceptions to the rule; and in some scenarios where there are factors favouring females over males. That male competitiveness in contrast to female backing-away is very deep-seated and not a cultural phenomenon is shown in its not merely cross-cultural but likely ancient occurrence: the same pattern is found even in extant hunter-gatherer (forager) societies (Apicella & Dreber, 2014). Even then, all the experimental and survey literature actually heavily understates what goes on in the real-world (in the jargon, the experiments are said to have little ecological validity). This is because what are being studied are one-off instances of competition rather than repeat competitive interactions, which have a growing impact over time – as we know males experience in the forming of dominance hierarchies. The first ever set of formal experiments to test the impact of just such iteration were not carried out until as recently as 2014, when David Gill and Victoria Prowse found that it produced a sex-differential in competitiveness far bigger still than had been found with non-iterated measures. Win or lose, males are spurred to be substantially even more competitive, whereas females still further reduce effort. In other words, whilst even repeat winning discourages females, winning is its own reward for males; and, furthermore, males are driven to convert losing into winning. Evidently, males have competitiveness in their bones, but for females competition appears to be problematic. The only thing that seems to damp down male competitiveness is heavy losing if also the stakes are high; but the effect is only for an instant. It too serves to further drive male competitiveness, by prompting men to 'cut their losses' and shift all their effort to some other competitive arena in which they're personally better suited. On the surface, males sometimes may look flaky, but it's very effective to confine your effort to where you discover your strength resides and to quickly abandon effort where you may be little better than middling, or pretty fine but not pre-eminent. Yes, herein lies the risk of putting your eggs in one basket, but risk-taking is an effective male strategy given the huge potential reproductive pay-offs – an 'alpha male' can monopolise sex in his local community to massively skew his contribution to the gene pool, which is something a female can never do.

Reflecting this is the very well-known starkly different character of the 'normal distribution' (the 'bell') curve of variation according to sex of almost any measurable effort, ability or achievement. Males overwhelmingly predominate at both extremes (the top and the bottom tails), in contrast to female predominance in the fat middle (at the median). Consequently, even for something regarding which on average men don't really perform any more strongly than do women – or even if females out-perform males (as in some female-sex-typical tasks) – there are, nonetheless, still far more males at and towards the top end of performance. Few spot the mirror image of there being also far more males at and towards the bottom end of performance. The male extremes cancel each other out to average the same or similar to female performance, albeit that the latter just sticks within the middle ground, not being too far either side of the dead centre. Males at and towards the bottom of the distribution have drawn the short straws on the 'genetic filter' stakes, are out of the reproductive running, and, through the evolved psychology from the biological imperative of 'policing' males, they are effectively invisible. This is why nobody notices the counterbalancing of the male 'geniuses' by the male 'dunces', and instead see the male high-performers vis-a-vis the merely averagely-performing females, and then think something must be awry between the sexes. On the contrary, all is hunky-dory between the sexes; it's merely that what goes on between males radically contrasts with what goes on between females. The general pattern of distribution of measures is itself a sex dichotomy indicating profound sex-specific core behaviour/cognition. It's a vivid visual rendition of the sex dichotomy re competitiveness.

The female backing-away – negative competitiveness – is the most interesting facet of the contrast between the sexes re competition. Fervent attempts to explain it away as something other than implicit non-competitiveness have all failed. A key notion here of ideologically addled 'social scientists' is that competitiveness is frowned upon in women and that in consequence women 'internalise' this as 'stereotype threat' (*sic*), from which they recoil (Iriberri & Rey-Biel, 2013), even though two recent attempts to test the 'theory' produced entirely contrary findings (Geraldes, Riedl & Strobel, 2011; Fryer, Levitt & List, 2008). Fatal to the 'theory' is that it isn't –

a theory. With any and every piece of evidence – even that which is mutually antagonistic – being invariably interpreted as supportive, its unfalsifiability is thereby revealed. When, finally, the 'theory' was critically reviewed, in 2012 by Gijsbert Stoet & David Geary, it was comprehensively refuted. They noted that the various studies didn't even feature a male 'control' group. For all the proponents of 'stereotype threat' (*sic*) knew, if data were available, then, on their assumptions, it might show men to be more impacted than women. Finding generic deeply flawed methodology, the authors conclude that there is little if any evidence at all for the supposed phenomenon. It's a similar convoluted notion to try to explain away unwelcome findings as is 'internalised misogyny' (*sic*), and about as plausible.

Another attempt to explain away lack of female competitiveness even at first glance looks like a mere re-statement that women are not competitive. It's the supposition that women would be as competitive as men if they chose, were it not for them being egalitarian compared to men. That's an odd claim given the firmly exclusionary nature of female sociality contrasting with the all-inclusivity of male wider grouping. That females are non-hierarchical does not mean that they are egalitarian. And being non-egalitarian does not mean that females are competitive other than in highly circumscribed ways. Most recently, the claim of female egalitarianism nullifying competitiveness has been refined into 'aheadness'-aversion (*sic*) (Bartling, Fehr, Marechal & Schunk, 2009); in other words, an antipathy to winning. Interestingly, the same study did *not* find a 'behindness'-aversion (*sic*) – a fear of losing. A fear of losing might suggest less an antipathy to competition per se than to the form of competition and what is was over; but an absence of concern about losing generically whilst also wanting to avoid being seen to put yourself above others reveals a profound non-competitiveness through an implicit attitude that being competitive would be irrelevant and not merely disadvantageous. Whilst competitiveness as physical aggressiveness potentially seriously compromises female reproduction, and most females surely view that as disadvantageous; the finding that females back away applies to competition of any form; even where there is no apparent potential for damage. Females are, then, generally – albeit with the exception of a clearly circumscribed arena – just plain non-competitive by default. We're back, it would seem, with an in-built avoidance by women of what is (that is, that they themselves would consider) unfeminine.

## SECTION 22

## CROSS-SEX, IT'S SEXUAL DISPLAY, NOT CONTEST: MEN ACT, WOMEN FLAUNT

Just what is going on here becomes clear in moving from looking at the sexes separately in their same-sex competitiveness to when men and women / boys and girls compete (supposedly) against each other; that is, to competition scenarios that are at least ostensibly between-sex. As we have seen, there is no such thing as competition, at least in earnest, that is between- rather than within-sex. Males would just signal deference – a pointed declining to engage in what would be inappropriate, meaningless dominance contest – or back off from female 'controlling' behaviour turning physically aggressive in sexual partnership contexts. So how is it, then, that in her above-cited review of last year, Muriel Niederle additionally finds that when they are up against women/girls, men/boys may actually *increase* their performance and/or choose a more competitive form of contest in comparison to how women/girls would behave? For the reason that this is an effective form of sexual display. Males put their mate-value on show in indicating dominance or potential dominance over other males; and, therefore, performance per se – in effect competitiveness against own or imagined other males' past or expected performance levels – is likely to be evoked in a between-sex context. In 2016, Arnaud Tognetti's team demonstrated this experimentally, concluding that "men adopt co-operative behaviours as a signalling strategy in the context of mate choice". This is not competitiveness towards the display target. It's a courtship or pre-courtship routine.

In many species, it appears that male dominance signalling – that is, the signals *divorced from the behaviour itself* – has been co-opted in evolution to function differently; as part of courtship.

It's an obvious development given that females sexually select males according to the males' dominance over other males. A female thus signalled can respond coyly to try to evoke more of it in a call-and-response loop of mutually testing ardour, that ratchets up into courtship, leading up to the possibility of sex. This male-female call-and-response routine is likely to be a non-conscious (implicitly cognitive) feature of male-female interaction generally, whether or not it is construable as courting. The dynamic here is all too readily recognised by women and girls, and is the basis of *the* biggest publishing phenomenon of all time: romance fiction – stories of a dominant (alpha male) hero and passive heroine. The hero can be ruthlessly nasty to other males in his dominance over them, whereas far from being dominant over the heroine he has no control over the lust if not a wider, deeper passion that the heroine evokes in him. The hero and heroine are together as if in a vortex imposed on them from outside (but actually it's just their own sexual imperatives, of course), to which both parties have been obliged to cede their will, and in sex the woman is simply 'taken'. Exaggerated into sado-masochism (though seemingly as a misrepresentation of a paraphilia), this explains why *Fifty Shades of Grey* sold in gargantuan quantities to women, despite being a strong contender for a prize as the world's worst-written novel.

Now, if males behave in a between-sex mode to sexually display by upping performance that would indicate a competitive aptitude, to elicit a female coy response, so that, in turn, is prompted more male sexual display … then females backing-off from being competitive would serve to allow *them* to display *their* own mate-value, so that *they* can initiate a (pre-)courtship call-and-response routine. The female display, instead of anything performance-based, is of their physical feminine attributes. They flaunt their bodies – shape can be best displayed in certain poses and types of movement. The key signal of female fertility is non-pregnancy and youth indicated by a small waist depth (front/back) in comparison to waist circumference (similar to the commonly cited waist-to-hip ratio, which experiment shows is less indicative than waist depth to circumference). This is best revealed in static poise or slow graceful movement, whereas vigorous movement does not show off the female body in a feminine way, and, furthermore, is or implies a female-sex-inappropriate pugnaciousness in a male-style competitiveness. Most blatantly, this is apparent when girls in school are playing even a female sport such as netball (where there can be no sense of unfavourable comparison with male performance). Old studies recorded that girls pause such physical activity when boys pass by, and instead adopt feminine poise and demeanour. [Presumably, there are no recent studies because nowadays nobody wants to be ostracised for revealing politically inconvenient data.] It's no surprise, then, that sporting activity usually is quickly relinquished by girls in school when it is no longer mandated, and not often taken up by women – heterosexual women, at least. The recent notion that it's because of puberty and bra problems is just to re-state the very reason it's an attempt to contradict. No surprise either, that the persistent 'public service' media heavy promotion of female sporting competitions corresponding to those of males continues to fail badly to attract a big audience. Team sports are particularly non-feminine – the regular comments and jibes about the high proportion of lesbian players are not without foundation; but, on the other hand, females who associate through a sport over a period of time might form a mass of heavily overlapping personal networks such that well integrated teams result. The female sport that is the sole exception in popularity is not just a non-team sport (as is golf, which again does not have a large audience) but the one sport that facilitates posing in feminine manner and graceful movement: tennis. The serve could have been designed as female sexual display, and in comparison to the men, even top women tennis players are so non-athletic in chasing down the ball as to appear nigh-on dainty. The BBC admitted (in 2016) focusing on the men's game because the women's is nothing like as exciting, with few 'stars' – even women at the very top of the sport are so uncompetitive relative to their male opposite numbers that rankings are highly volatile. Seeded women can be almost all out of major tournaments by the third round.

The polarisation between the sexes re competitiveness when ostensibly men and women are pitched against each other, is, then, an implicit (pre-)courtship dynamic. But it's easy to pretend otherwise through other factors which interfere with – 'confound' – the data in experimental studies, having being introduced (and often not unwittingly) but then not taken into account. Most obviously, the sex-appropriateness or typicality of a competition task and/or context may be crucial. You hardly can make a sexual display of something that belongs in the domain of the opposite sex; and you are more likely to utilise for sexual display an activity which is appropriate for your sex than something that is 'sex-neutral'. Whereas the standard female 'backing away' behaviour is apparent in no improvement in performance even if the task/context is made female sex-appropriate/sex-typical; males may join females in backing away from competition and reducing their performance if the task/context is switched to one that is female-appropriate/typical. At the same time, though, males are more eager to engage in competition and increase their performance with a change from a sex-neutral to a male-appropriate/typical task/context. Another important confound is 'priming' – making more psychologically salient – either the sex of participants and/or that it is a competition. This will impact on implicit cognition and likely also on more focused explicit cognition (an awareness of what you're thinking). This is likely to undermine male performance as sexual display through invoking an intuitive 'chivalry' stemming from evolved deference – signalled non-engagement in dominance behaviour. In consequence, men are then likely to reduce performance and/or avoid choosing a competition option. No such effect would be expected to be evident in women, and indeed this is the case, except for some situations where women are together in a same-sex pair or group and faced with a male or a male group (Ivanova-Stenzel & Kübler, 2005). The authors interpret this as a risk-averse perception of a male 'out-group' threat prompting greater female-female co-operation which as a by-product ups performance. Yet even if this interpretation were valid, the co-operation does not look to be in the service of competitiveness, but instead threat reduction by dilution of exposure, akin to herding behaviour to minimise the risk of individual predation. The main problem with the notion here of a threat is that this is something males don't pose to women. An alternative and more likely understanding of what is going on here is simply that male presence primes female same-sex in-grouping – remembering that girls/women have a fourfold same-sex preference in choosing in-group members.

All of these confounds are liable to be misconstrued as revealing between-sex competitiveness – even, in some scenarios, that women are more competitive than are men – when actually they show nothing of the kind. [You can find a discussion of this, looking at individual papers to show the various sleight of hand, in my paper on competitiveness.]

## Section 23

## The Myth Of 'Sexual Conflict': It's Actually A Within-Sex Phenomenon

With between-sex competitiveness biting the dust along with between-sex dominance/submission, and also male 'mate-guarding' being turned on its head to be replaced with female 'control'; then the whole supposed 'war of the sexes' in even any ideological sense is sent packing; never mind, surely, 'sexual conflict' having any scientific basis. Actually, however, there remains an abstract notion that a conflict between the sexes is primitively foundational, in the concept of 'sexual conflict', as it is used in biological sciences. But whenever it's employed it does not take much investigation to see that it resolves to *within*-sex competition. Indeed, within-sex competition is explicitly included as part of 'sexual conflict', as Greg Gorelik & Todd Shackelford (2011) outline in their review of the various supposed manifestations of the phenomenon. This renders the concept a misnomer. The 'sexual conflict' literature was reviewed earlier (in 1999) by Catherine Lessells, who concedes that: "the extent to which these behaviours are adaptations to male same-sex competition or to conflict with females over mate choice is not clear". Within-sex competition is a full and more parsimonious understanding, leaving 'sexual conflict' a superfluous analysis and conceptual error: a pejorative understanding all too apparent as an inappropriate importation to science from contemporary politics.

Supposedly, there is a between-sex 'arms race' in respect of evolutionary adaptations, that in one sex in some way are an attempt to get round the mate-choice criteria of the opposite sex, and then vice-versa in the attempt to counteract this. Indeed, on the surface this is just what seems to be in play. But the supposed 'arms race' actually is a progressive ratcheting-up of overall reproductive efficiency of the reproductive-group as a whole – which, as previously mentioned, is a proper understanding in terms of population-genetics / population structure / 'lineage-selection'; not 'group-selection'. Any adaptation that confers some advantage to males in terms of sexual access / reproductive output inevitably is a focus of male-male competition and competitive selection by females. It is in the female interest to prefer those males possessing such an advantage, and effectively to compete against other females in this respect. That an adaptation may be seen as some sort of 'cheating' – 'dishonest-signalling' – does not alter this, because the facility to be able to get round opposite-sex mate-choice criteria in this way *itself* is a quality requiring the very kind of attributes that are an expression of male 'good genes' – even if it is just an indication of a pugnacious and fearless attitude. So females do not lose out through choosing males with these types of successful new adaptations: the genetic underpinning is passed on to their offspring males who will in turn be more successful in reproducing. Females compete with *each other* to better detect 'dishonest signalling'. Males can respond by refining the 'dishonest signalling' so as to compete with other males. The ratcheting-up of 'dishonest-signalling' and corresponding 'dishonest-signal detection' is a merry-go-round requiring such refined qualities in both sexes that mate-choice actually becomes ever more discerning: ever more an accurate assessment of male 'good genes'. In other words, 'dishonest signalling' paradoxically becomes, through the lengths taken to refine it, itself 'honest signalling' of the male's genetic attributes. Far from compromising the female, it facilitates and refines her accurate mate choice.

This perspective is recognised by reviewers of the 'sexual conflict' perspective, at least to an extent. Monique Borgerhoff Mulder & Kriston Rauch (2009) realise that: "More fundamentally, of course, the identification of winners and losers is a flawed pursuit. There are winners and losers in each sex. … Furthermore, the costs and benefits of mating systems are not distributed homogenously within each sex; some males are big winners and others are big losers. … Generally, we should think of sexually antagonistic contests as dynamic and ongoing. In this view, neither sex 'wins', at least not for more than a short spell. … winners being individuals who are particularly successful not only in manipulating or controlling the behavior of the other sex, but in competing with their own sex". Gorelik & Shackelford likewise start to get there in the end, when they state: "… as the co-evolutionary arms race between men and women advanced, enhancement of deceptive tactics placed women under selection pressure to be attracted to men who were skilled at deception (as these men were more likely to sire reproductively successful offspring). In this way, instances of sexual conflict may sometimes evolve into instances of sexual cooperation".

Reviewers have come to realise, then, that in moving away from a snapshot view of one sex being put upon by the other, that there is a balance between the sexes in a constructive dynamic. Yet having partly corrected the conceptualisation, discussion veers back to remain in terms of the 'sexual conflict' label and concept simply through the need for the shared familiar terminology without which discussion would be at cross purposes. Thus is allowed a continuing failure to drill down further to the underlying dynamic, even though thinking is shifting away from envisaging a between-sex conflict to a between-sex synergy, with the conflict left within-sex.

What might seem to be a stark form of 'sexual conflict' that cannot resolve within-sex is infanticide – the occurrence, in several species (as, famously, for lions), where a male who usurps another male in gaining regular sexual access to a female, kills very young offspring so that the female stops lactating and returns to menstrual cycling, and is then available for impregnation. This could not be more clearly an immediate major cost to the female, and yet … thereafter it's a benefit. Actually, it's not hard to see why. The usurper necessarily is the more dominant male, who is then in place to contribute his superior complement of genes to the female's next set off offspring. Yes, she has lost offspring, but not only have they been immediately replaced, but replaced by offspring of better quality. This can be decisive, because in species where infanticide occurs offspring survivability is low. In the case of the lion, the cubs are highly vulnerable not just to predation but particularly to starvation, especially as they become large but still incapable of successful hunting. The female is most likely to lose her offspring just at the very point they are approaching independence, after she has invested a huge amount of time and effort. The advent of a superior male to sire her offspring can tip the odds regarding offspring viability sufficient to make all the difference. In this quality-over-quantity game, the upshot is that the female's overall reproductive output is likely to have been notably enhanced. Consequently, females will have evolved to adapt to this reality, and to have no problem – implicitly – with the loss of offspring conceived via the vanquished male and to fully accept the usurping male with the better reproductive prospect this brings. Pulling out the lens still further, the loser here is not the female but the vanquished male. He has lost, to the usurping male, both a set of offspring *and* the future prospect of offspring; at least with this female. So what at first sight is a between-sex issue once again actually resolves to one that is *within*-sex.

Where the 'sexual conflict' notion and mindset appears, at least on the surface, less a political imposition than scientifically real is when we get right down to the level of the gene. There are genes or alleles that are selected because they provide a benefit to one sex only, or at the same time may even be detrimental to the other. This might seem incontrovertible 'sexual conflict', but as well as the same principles applying to the underlying genetics as to how they manifest in behaviour or morphology, 'sexual conflict' hardly can occur if the gene is not expressed or expressed differently in the other sex. An area of current rapid discovery is of the different gene expression according to sex: either in a sex-biased way (by different degrees), or sex-specifically (chalk and cheese). Clearly, this would avoid any 'sexual conflict' issue. Inasmuch as it isn't avoided, there is no reason why at this level too there isn't the same sort of within-sex competition and mutual ratcheting-up in the service of ever greater reproductive efficiency.

It used to be thought that sex itself initially arose through 'sexual conflict' – the question of how sex arose is a separate one from how sex was then maintained to be selected to 'fixation' by being co-opted in the evolutionary process in the 'genetic filter' function. As is fathomed from phylogenetic (evolutionary tree) data and a number of extant 'primitive' species thought to be evolutionary 'throwbacks'; ancestrally, sex cells (gametes) were all identical. They are said to be isogamous (by which is meant iso*metric*: all of the same size). In other words, there were no distinct mating types: no male and female. Anisogamy – differently sized gametes, with the larger being by this definition denoted the female – has been assumed to be the result of one of two forms of 'sexual conflict': either intra-genomic (at gene level) or a 'parasitism' of male gametes on female. But far from only one gamete type being advantaged at the expense of the other, anisogamy is now shown in models to produce increased fitness for both resulting mating types. Anisogamy evolves if large zygotes (the product of fusing two gametes) are favoured and the difference in gamete sizes maximises the rate at which gametes encounter each other, and hence the number of zygotes produced (Roughgarden & Iyer 2011; Iyer 2009). This usually would be the case, in that large zygotes make sense as they take considerably less time to grow into an adult; and the rate that gametes meet would be highest where one gamete type is a lot more mobile and in greater numbers compared to the other, which necessarily is sedentary through its containing the tissue and resources needed to produce a large zygote.

As well as the notion of 'sexual conflict' being inapplicable to anisogamy, it's irrelevant to a new, alternative theory as to how sex initially arose, advanced notably by Nick Lane, of 'mitonuclear co-evolution' (Hadjivasiliou et al, 2012). Lane posits that sex once existed (and in some species still exists) despite there being no size distinction between the gametes; that is, before anisogamy developed. It concerns the genes controlling the structures within the cell responsible for meeting all energy requirements (the mitochondria). Uniquely, these genes are both in the cell nucleus and also the body (cytoplasm) of the cell, causing problems of mutual coordination. How these have evolved to work closely together needs to be preserved in a way that the process of recombination in sex would completely disrupt. Consequently, they are always inherited down one side of the lineage – only via females.

The concept of 'sexual conflict' looks less healthy than ever, if not moving from being on life support to the mortuary slab.

# Section 24

## Coda: The Symbosis Of The Sexes

To many, especially those having little familiarity with biology, the foregoing outline of men/women may come across as hard to believe, but it's what researchers easily pick up and very much what anyone readily can see around them once they know what they are looking at, having dropped the false frame with which they've been mis-educated into wrapping everything. Without a biological 'bottom-up' perspective, the data re the sexes, men/women, is sure to continue to confuse. It can be manipulated to seem to bolster those who peddle the tired and inherently contradictory notions of social constructivism and extreme-feminism: that any seeming shortfall or aberration in women's performance or behaviour in comparison to men must be the result of prejudice towards women and inappropriate go-getting by men. On the contrary, the whole picture and its every facet stems from the very different basis of how we think and behave according to sex, as the 'bottom-up' biological outline here espoused both gets underneath and provides the guide to how it manifests.

There is not and never has been a 'war of the sexes' as nowadays this is meant, rather than the endearing foibles of miscommunication everyone considered comic and life-enriching, to which the phrase 'the war of the sexes' formerly referred. The sexes in fact beautifully complement each other, as everyone intuitively well understands. Given what science so very clearly reveals – and that humans hardly could not have always intuited; then it seems astonishing anyone could ever have thought otherwise.

Those who tell you that men and women are in essence at loggerheads, with some 'power' imbalance dividing them, are either charlatans with an elitist/separatist backlash political agenda against people en mass, or 'useful idiots' for that line in parroting it. Not merely extremism, contemporary ideology is a fact-free, in fact counter-factual – fact-inverting – zone, through the imperative to grotesquely twist reality to fit the narrow political 'social justice' battle (as I outlined at the outset) of neo-Marxian replacement of the 'bosses versus workers' by 'woman versus man'. Cutting through the thick layers of contemporary ideological obfuscation and instead looking to science, it could not be clearer that male and female generically, not excluding men and women specifically, are in perfectly complementary relationship.

A symbiosis.

# REFERENCES

Abbott, D. H., Keverne, E. B., Bercovitch, F. B., Shively, C. A., Mendoza, S. P., Saltzman, W., Snowdon, C. T., Ziegler, T. E., Banjevic, M., Garland, T. & Sapolsky, R. M. (2003). Are subordinates always stressed? A comparative analysis of rank differences in cortisol levels among primates. *Hormones and Behavior,* 43(1), 67-82. doi:10.1016/S0018-506X(02)00037-5

Abed, R. T. (1998). The Sexual Competition Hypothesis For Eating Disorders. *British Journal of Medical Psychology,* 71(4), 525-547. doi: 10.1111/j.2044-8341.1998.tb01007.x

Adler, P. & Adler, P. (1998) *Peer Power: Preadolescent Culture and Identity.* Rutgers University Press.

Agrawal, A. F. (2001). Sexual selection and the maintenance of sexual reproduction. *Nature,* 411, 692-695. doi: 10.1038/35079590

Ali, N. (2012). Blog – nellyali: Ramblings between London and Cairo FGM: Mutilating the Female Spirit. 8/6/2012. http://nellyali.wordpress.com/2012/06/08/fgm-mutilating-the-female-spirit

Anderson, C., Spataro, S. E. & Flynn, F. J. (2008). Personality and organizational culture as determinants of influence. *Journal of Applied Psychology,* 93(3), 702-710. doi: 10.1037/0021-9010.93.3.702

Anderson, K. L. (2002). Perpetrator or victim? Relationships between intimate partner violence and well being. *Journal or Marriage and the Family,* 64, 851-863. doi: 10.1111/j.1741-3737.2002.00851.x

Apicella, C. L. & Dreber, A. (2014). Sex Differences in Competitiveness: Hunter-Gatherer Women and Girls Compete Less in Gender-Neutral and Male-Centric Tasks. *Adaptive Human Behavior and Physiology.* [On-line publication only] http://link.springer.com/article/10.1007/s40750-014-0015-z

Archer, J. (1999). Assessment of the reliability of the conflict tactics scales: A meta-analytic review. *Journal of Interpersonal Violence,* 14, 1263-1289 doi: 10.1177/088626099014012003

Archer, J. (2000). Sex differences in aggression between heterosexual partners: A meta-analytic review. *Psychological Bulletin,* 126(5), 651-680. doi: 10.1037//0033-2909.126.5.651

Atmar, W. (1991). On the role of males. *Animal behaviour,* 41(2), 195-20. doi: 10.1016/S0003-3472(05)80471-3

Bailey, D. H., Winegard, B., Oxford, J. & Geary, D. C. (2012). Sex Differences in In-Group Cooperation Vary Dynamically with Competitive Conditions and Outcomes. *Evolutionary Psychology* (http://www.epjournal.net), 10(1), 102-119. doi:10.1177/147470491201000112

Baker, R. R. & Bellis, M. A. (1995). *Human sperm competition: Copulation, masturbation, and infidelity.* Chapman and Hall, London.

Baker, J. M., Liu, N., Cui, X., Vrticka, P., Saggar, M., Hadi Hosseini, S. M. & Reiss, A. L. (2016). Sex differences in neural and behavioral signatures of cooperation revealed by fNIRS hyperscanning. *Scientific Reports,* 6, 26492. doi:10.1038/srep26492

Bangasser, D. A. et al (2010). Sex differences in Corticotropin-Releasing Factor receptor signaling and trafficking: potential role in female vulnerability to stress-related psychopathology. *Molecular Psychiatry,* 15(9), 877-904. doi: 10.1038/mp.2010.66

Bartling, B., Fehr, E., Marechal, M. A. & Schunk, D. (2009). Egalitarianism and Competitiveness. *American Economic Review (Papers and Proceedings),* 99(2), 93-98. doi=10.1257/aer.99.2.93

Bates, E. A., Graham-Kevan, N. & Archer, J. (2014). Testing predictions from the male control theory of men's partner violence. *Aggressive Behavior,* 40(1), 42-55. doi: 10.1002/ab.21499

Bateup, H. S., Booth, A., Shirtcliff, E.A. & Granger, D. A. (2002). Testosterone, cortisol and women's competition. *Evolution & Human Behavior,* 23, 181-192. doi: 10.1016/j.yhbeh.2016.04.004

Baumeister, R. (2002). Cultural Suppression of Female Sexuality. *Review of General Psychology,* 6(2), 166-203. doi: 10.1037//1089-2680.6.2.166

Bedau, M. A. & Humphreys, P. (2008). *Emergence: Contemporary Readings in Philosophy and Science.* MIT Press.

Bell, R. & Buchner, A. (2009). Enhanced source memory for names of cheaters. *Evolutionary Psychology,* 7(2), 317-330. doi: 10.1177/147470490900700213

Benenson, J. F., Stella, S. & Ferranti, A. (2015). Sex differences in human gregariousness. *PeerJ* 3 e974. doi: 10.7717/peerj.974

Benenson, J. F., Markovits, H., Hultgren, B., Nguyen, T., Bullock, G & Wrangham, R. (2013). Social Exclusion: More Important to Human Females Than Males. *PLoS ONE,* 8(2), e55851. doi: 10.1371/journal.pone.0055851

Bernstein, I. S., Judge, P. G. & Ruehlmann, T. E. (1993). Sex differences in adolescent rhesus monkey (Macaca mulatta) behavior. *American Journal of Primatology,* 31(3), 197-210. doi: 10.1002/ajp.1350310305

Blake, C. F. (1994). Foot-binding in Neo-Confucian China and the Appropriation of Female Labor. *Signs,* 19(3), 676-712. [p682]

Bologna, M. J., Waterman, C. K. & Dawson, L. J. (1987). Violence in Gay Male and Lesbian Relationships: Implications for practitioners and policy makers. [Paper Presented at the Third National Conference for Family Violence Researchers, Durham, NH.]

Bonnefon, J. F., Hopfensitz, A. & De Neys, W. (2013). The modular nature of trustworthiness detection. *Journal of Experimental Psychology: General,* 142, 143-150. doi: 10.1037/a0028930

Booth, A., Granger, D. A., Mazur, A. & Kivlighan, K. T. (2006). Testosterone and social behavior. *Social Forces,* 85(1), 167-191. doi: 10.1353/sof.2006.0116

Borgeroff Mulder, M. & Rauch, K. L. (2009). Sexual conflict in humans: variations and solutions. *Evolutionary Anthropology,* 18, 201-214. doi: 10.1002/evan

Boulanger, L., Pannetier, M., Gall, L., Allais-Bonnet, A., Elzaiat. M., Le Bourhis, D., Daniel, N., Richard, C., Cotinot, C., Ghyselinck, N. B. & Pailhoux. E. (2014). FOXL2 is a female sex-determining gene in the goat. *Current Biology,* 24(4), 404-408. doi: 10.1016/j.cub.2013.12.039

Bronselaer, G., Schober, J. M., Meyer-Bahlburg, H. F., T'Sjoen, G., Vlietinck, R. & Hoebeke, P. B. (2013). Male circumcision decreases penile sensitivity as measured in a large cohort. *British Journal of Urology International,* 111, 820-827. doi: 10.1111/j.1464-410X.2012.11761.x

Brotherton, P. & Komers, P. (2003). Monogamy: Mating Strategies and Partnerships. 42-58, in *Birds, Humans and Other Mammals* (ed Reichard, U. & Boesch, C.). Cambridge University Press,

Brown, B. B. & Klute, C. (2003, 2008). Friendships Cliques and Crowds, in Adams & Berzonsky (ed), *Handbook of Adolescent Development.* Blackwell.

Buunk, A. P. & Massar, K. (2012). Intra-sexual competition among males: Competitive towards men, prosocial towards women. *Personality and Individual Differences,* 52, 818-821. doi: 10.1016/j.paid.2012.01.010

Campos, J. L., Charlesworth, B. & Haddrill, P. R. (2012). Molecular evolution in non-recombining regions of the Drosophila melanogaster genome. *Genome Biology and Evolution,* 4, 278-288. doi: 10.1093/gbe/evs010

Capaldi, D. M. & Owen, L. D. (2001). Physical aggression in a community sample of at-risk young couples: Gender comparisons for high frequency, injury, and fear. *Journal of Family Psychology,* 15, 425-440. doi: 10.1037//0893-3200.15.3.425

Carroll, S. (2011). Downward Causation. *Discover* Magazine, August 1. http://blogs.discovermagazine.com/cosmicvariance/2011/08/01/downward-causation/

Chandola, T., Kuper, H., Singh-Manoux, A., Bartley, M. & Marmot, M. G. (2004). The effect of control at home on CHD events in the Whitehall II study: Gender differences in psychosocial domestic pathways to social inequalities in CHD. *Social Science & Medicine,* 58(8), 1501-1509. doi: 10.1016/S0277-9536(03)00352-6

Chapais, B. (2011). The Evolutionary History of Pair-bonding and Parental Collaboration. Chapter 3 in *The Oxford Handbook of Evolutionary Family Psychology* (ed Salmon, C. & Shackelford, T. K.). Oxford University Press.

Chapais, B. (2008). *Primeval Kinship: How Pair Bonding Gave Birth to Human Society.* Harvard University Press.

Chu, J. (2014). *When Boys Become Boys: Development, Relationships, and Masculinity.* NYU Press.

Cochas, A., Yoccoz, N. G., Da Silva, A., Goossens, B. & Allainé, D. (2006). Extra-pair paternity in the monogamous alpine marmot (Marmota marmota): the roles of social setting and female mate choice. *Behavioral Ecology & Sociobiology,* 59, 597-605. doi: 10.1007/s00265-005-0086-8

Colarelli, S. M., Spranger, J. L. & Hechanova, R. (2006). Women, power, and sex composition in small groups: An evolutionary perspective. *Journal of Organizational Behavior,* 27(2), 163-184. doi: 10.1002/job.350

Coleman, V. E. (1990). Violence between lesbian couples: A between groups comparison. Unpublished doctoral dissertation. University Microfilms International 9109022.

Coleman, K. & Straus, M. (1986). Marital power, conflict, and violence in a nationally

representative sample of American couples. *Violence and Victims,* 1, 141-157.

Colombelli-Négrel, D., Schlotfeldt, B. E. & Kleindorfer, S. (2009). High levels of extra-pair paternity in Superb Fairy-wrens in South Australia despite low frequency of auxiliary males. *Emu – Australian Ornithology,* 109(4), 300-304. doi: 10.1071/MU09035

Connolly, J., Furman, W. & Konarsky, R. (2000). The role of peers in the emergence of heterosexual romantic relationships in adolescence. *Child Development,* 71(5), 1395-1408. doi: 10.1111/1467-8624.00235

Cook, J. L. & Cook, G. (on-line update 2015). Gender Segregation Among Childhood Friends, 423-425. From (2009) *Child Development Principles and Perspectives.* Pearson Allyn Bacon Prentice Hall.

Corby, S. & Stanworth, C. (2009). A price worth paying?: Women and work – choice, constraint or satisficing. *Equal Opportunities International,* 28(2), 162-168. doi:10.1108/02610150910937907

Cotten, C., McIntyre, F. & Price, J. (2015). Which explanations for gender differences in competition are consistent with a simple theoretical model? Social Science Research Network. http://papers.ssrn.com/sol3/papers.cfm?abstract_id=2556408] doi: 10.1016/j.socec.2015.09.005

Cross, C. P., Tee, W. & Campbell, A. (2011). Gender symmetry in intimate aggression: an effect of intimacy or target sex? *Aggressive Behavior,* 37(3), 268–277. doi: 10.1002/ab.20388

Cross, C. P. & Campbell, A. (2012). The effect of intimacy and target sex on direct aggression: Further evidence. *Aggressive Behavior,* 38, 272-280. doi: 10.1002/ab.21430

Crowley, J. J., De Villena, P-M. et al (2015). Analyses of allele-specific gene expression in highly divergent mouse crosses identifies pervasive allelic imbalance. *Nature Genetics,* 47, 353-360. doi: 10.1038/ng.3222

Cummins, D. D. (1996). Dominance hierarchies and the evolution of human reasoning. *Minds & Machines,* 6, 463-480. doi: 10.1007/BF00389654

Cummins, D. D. (1996b). Evidence of deontic reasoning in 3- and 4-year-olds. *Memory & Cognition,* 24, 823-829. doi: 10.3758/BF03201105

Cummins, D. D. (1996c). Evidence for the innateness of deontic reasoning. *Mind & Language,* 11, 160-190. doi: 10.1111/j.1468-0017.1996.tb00039.x

Cummins, D. D. (1999a). Cheater detection is modified by social rank. *Evolution and Human Behavior,* 20, 229-248. doi: 10.1016/S1090-5138(99)00008-2

Cummins, D. D. (2005). Dominance, status, and social hierarchies. In Buss, D. M. (ed) *The Handbook of Evolutionary Psychology*, 676-697. Wiley.

Cummins, D. D. (2013). Deontic Reasoning as a Target of Selection: Reply to Astington and Dack (2013). *Journal of Experimental Child Psychology,* 116(4), 970-974. doi: 10.1016/j.jecp.2013.03.005

Dasgupta, S. D. (1999). Just like men? A Critical view of violence by women. In Shephard & Pence (eds) *Coordinating community responses to domestic violence*, 195-222. Thousand Oaks CA Sage Publication.

David-Barrett, T., Rotkirch, A., Carney, J., Behncke Izquierdo, I., Krems, J.A., Townley, D., McDaniell, E., Byrne-Smith, A. & Dunbar, R. I. M. (2015). Women Favour Dyadic Relationships, but Men Prefer Clubs: Cross-Cultural Evidence from Social Networking. *PLoS ONE,* 10(3), e0118329. doi: 10.1371/journal.pone.0118329

Dawkins, R. (1976). *The Selfish Gene.* Oxford University Press.

Dawkins, R. (1989). *The Extended Phenotype: The Long Reach of the Gene.* Oxford Paperbacks.

Dawkins, R. (2004). Extended Phenotype – But Not Too Extended. A Reply to Laland, Turner and Jablonka. *Biology & Philosophy,* 19(3), 377-396.

De Castillejo, I. C. (1973, repub 1997). *Knowing Woman: A Feminine Psychology.* Shambhala US.

De Zavala, A. G., Cichocka, A. & Bilewicz, M. (2013). The Paradox of In-group Love: Narcissistic and Genuine Positive Group Regard Have Reverse Effects on Out-Group Attitudes. *Journal of Personality,* 81(1), 16-28.

Deaner, R. O., Lowen, A., Rogers, W. & Saksa, E. (2015). Does the sex difference in competitiveness decrease in selective sub-populations? A test with intercollegiate distance runners. PeerJ 3 e884. doi: 10.7717/peerj.884

Degirmencioglu, S. M., Urberg, K. A., Tolson, J. M. & Richard, P. (1998). Adolescent friendship networks: Continuity and change over the school years. *Merrill-Palmer Quarterly,* 44(3), 313-337.

Del Giudice, M. (2009). Sex, attachment, and the development of reproductive strategies. *Behavioral & Brain Sciences,* 32(1), 1-21. doi: 10.1017/S0140525X09000016

Del Giudice, M., Booth, T. & Irwing, P. (2012). The distance between Mars and Venus: Measuring global sex differences in personality. *PLoS ONE,* 7, e29265. doi: 10.1371/journal.pone.0029265

Dennett, D. C. (1996). *Darwin's Dangerous Idea: Evolution and the Meanings of Life.* Penguin.

Dennett, D. C. (2003). *Freedom Evolves.* Penguin.

Desmarais, S. L., Reeves, K. A., Nicholls, T. L., Telford, R. P. & Fiebert, M. S. (2012b). Prevalence of physical violence in intimate relationships: part 2. Rates of male and female perpetration. *Partner Abuse,* 3(2), 170-198. doi: 10.1891/1946-6560.3.2.170

Desoto, M. C. & Salinas, M. (2015). Neuroticism and Cortisol: The Importance of Checking for Sex Differences. *Psychoneuroendocrinology,* 62, 174-179. doi: 10.1016/j.psyneuen.2015.07.608

DeWall, C. N., Gillath, O., Pressman, S. D., Black, L. L., Bartz, J., Moskovitz, J. & Stetler, D. A. (2014). When the Love Hormone Leads to Violence: Oxytocin Increases Intimate Partner Violence Inclinations Among High Trait Aggressive People. *Social Psychological and Personality Science,* XX(X), 1-6. doi:10.1177/1948550613516876

Dickins, T. E. & Dickins, J. A. (2008). Mother nature's tolerant ways: Why non-genetic inheritance has nothing to do with evolution. *New Ideas in Psychology,* 26(1), 41-54. DOI: 10.1016/j.newideapsych.2007.03.004

Dickins, T. E. (2005). On the Aims of Evolutionary Theory. A book review of Odling-Smee, J. J., Laland, K. N. & Feldman, M. W. (2003). Niche Construction: The Neglected Process in Evolution. *Evolutionary Psychology* 2005, 3. *human-nature.com/ep* doi:10.1177/147470490500300107

Dixon, L. (2012). [Personal email] "What is remarkable is the high proportion of men injured by their partners: the figures are 38% from a meta-analysis of 20 studies (Archer, 2000) and 35% from a more recent analysis of 14 studies (Straus, 2011). From the same perspective it is also remarkable that such a high percentage of men are killed by their partners (23% according to the Home Office figures cited by the Respect authors). Based on size and strength differences, a figure of around 95% would be expected in both cases."

Dugatkin, L. E. & Earley, R. L. (2004). Individual recognition, dominance hierarchies and winner and loser effects. *Proceedings of the Royal Society of London, Biological Sciences,* 271, 1537-1540. DOI: 10.1098/rspb.2004.2777

Dunbar, R. I. M. (2012). *The Science of Love and Betrayal.* Faber and Faber.

Dunham, Y., Baron, A. S. & Banaji, M. R. (2015). The development of implicit gender attitudes. *Developmental Science.* doi: 10.1111/desc.12321

Dunphy, D. (1963). The social structure of urban adolescent peer groups. *Sociometry,* 26(2). Reprinted in Grinder, R. E. (1969). *Studies in Psychology,* 11.

Dutton, D. G. (2012). The case against the role of gender in intimate partner violence. *Aggression and Violent Behavior,* 17(1), 99-100. doi: 10.1016/j.avb.2011.09.002

Eagly, A. H., Mladinic, A. & Otto, S. (1991). Are women evaluated more favorably than men? An analysis of attitudes, beliefs and emotions. *Psychology of Women Quarterly,* 15(2), 203-216. doi:10.1111/j.1471-6402.1991.tb00792.x

Ehrensaft, M. K. & Vivian, D. (1999). Is partner aggression related to appraisals of coervice control by a partner? *Journal of Family Violence,* 14, 251-266. doi:10.1023/A:1022862332595

Eisenmann, R. (2003). Forgetting to use birth control: Unwanted pregnancies support evolutionary psychology theory. *Journal of Evolutionary Psychology,* 24, 30-34.

European Science Foundation. (2008). The New Role of the Extended Phenotype in Evolutionary Biology. [ESF Explanatory Workshop, Copenhagen, Denmark, 2-5 November.]

Fabes, R. A., Martin, C. L. & Hanish, L. D. (2004). The next 50 years: Considering gender as a context for understanding young children's peer relationships. *Merrill-Palmer Quarterly,* 50(3), 260-273.

Fedigan, L. M. (1992). Dominance and Alliance: Chapter 7 of *Primate Paradigms: Sex Roles and Social Bonds.* University of Chicago Press.

Felson, R. B. & Cares, A. C. (2005) Gender and the seriousness of assaults on intimate partners and other victims. *Journal of Marriage and Family,* 67(5), 1182-1195. doi: 10.1111/j.1741-3737.2005.00209.x

Felson, R. B. & Outlaw, M. C. (2007). The control motive and marital violence. *Violence and Victims,* 22(4), 387-408. doi: 10.1891/088667007781553964

Fessler, D. M. & Navarrete, C. D. (2004). Third-party attitudes toward sibling incest, evidence for Westermarck's hypotheses. *Evolution & Human Behavior,* 25, 277-294.

Fiddick, L. & Cummins, D. D. (2001). Reciprocity in ranked relationships: Does social structure influence social reasoning? *Journal of Bioeconomics,* 3, 149-170. doi: 10.1023/A:1020572212265

Fiebert. M. (2014). References examining assaults by women on their spouses or male partners: an annotated bibliography. *Sexuality and Culture,* 18(2), 405-467. doi: 10.1007/s12119-013-9194-1

Fischer-Shofty, M., Levkovitz, Y. & Shamay-Tsoory, S. G. (2012). Oxytocin facilitates accurate perception of competition in men and kinship in women. *Social Cognitive & Affective Neuroscience,* 8(3), 313-317. doi: 10.1093/scan/nsr100

Fisher, H. E. (1989). Evolution of human serial pair-bonding. *American Journal of Physical Anthropology,* 78(3), 331-354. doi: 10.1002/ajpa.1330780303

Fisher, H. E. (1994). *Anatomy of Love: The Natural history of mating, marriage and why we stray.* Ballantine Books.

Fouts, H. N., Hallam, R. A. & Purandare, S. (2013). Gender Segregation in Early-Childhood Social Play among the Bofi Foragers and Bofi Farmers in Central Africa. *American Journal of Play,* 5(3), 333-356.

Fryer, R., Levitt, S. & List, J. (2008). Exploring the impact of financial incentives on stereotype threat: evidence from a pilot study. *American Economic Review: Papers & Proceedings,* 98(2), 370-375. doi: 10.1257/aer.98.2.370

Galaaen, O. S. (2006). The Disturbing Matter of Downward Causation: A Study of the Exclusion Argument and its Causal Explanatory Presuppositions. PhD dissertation, University of Oslo. https://www.duo.uio.no/bitstream/handle/10852/24951/the_disturbing_matter.pdf?sequence=1

Gammie, S. C., D'Anna, K. L., Lee, G. & Stevenson, S. A. (2008). Role of corticotrophin releasing factor-related peptides in the neural regulation of maternal defense. In *Neurobiology of the Parental Brain* (ed) Bridges, R. S. Academic Press.

Gangestad, S. W. & Thornhill, R. (2008). Human Oestrus. *Proceedings of the Royal Society (Biological Sciences),* 275(1638), 991-1000. doi: 10.1098/rspb.2007.1425

Geary, D. C. & Bailey, D. H. (2011). Reflections on the Human Family. Chapter 21 in *The Oxford Handbook of Evolutionary Family Psychology* (ed Salmon, C. & Shackelford, T. K.) Oxford University Press.

George, M. J. (2003). Invisible touch. *Aggression & Violent Behavior,* 8(1), 22-60. doi: 10.1016/S1359-1789(01)00048-9

Geraldes, D., Riedl, A. & Strobel, M. (2011). Sex and performance under competition: Is there a stereotype threat shadow? [Presentation to the European Economic Association & Econometric Society, Oslo, 25-29 August.] http://web.stanford.edu/group/SITE/archive/SITE_2011/2011_segment_7/2011_segment_7_papers/geraldes.pdf

Giallombardo, R. (1966). *Society of Women: a Study of Women's Prison.* John Wiley & Sons, New York.

Gill, G. & Prowse, V. (2014). Gender differences and dynamics in competition: The role of luck. *Quantitative Economics,* 5(2), 351-376. doi: 10.3982/QE309

Gilman, T. L., DaMert, J. P., Meduri, J.D. & Jasnow, A.M. (2015). Grin1 deletion in CRF neurons sex-dependently enhances fear, sociability, and social stress responsivity. *Psychoneuroendocrinology,* 58, 33-45. doi: 10.1016/j.psyneuen.2015.04.010

Goodwin, M. H. (2002). Exclusion in girls' peer groups: ethnographic analysis of language practices on the playground. *Human Development,* 45, 392-415. doi: 10.1159/000066260

Goodwin, S. & Rudman, L. (2004). Gender differences in automatic in-group bias: Why do women like women more than men like men? *Social Psychology,* 87(4), 494-509. doi: 10.1037/0022-3514.87.4.494

Gorelik, G. & Shackelford, T. K. (2011). Human sexual conflict from molecules to culture. *Evolutionary Psychology,* 9, 564-587. doi: 10.1177/147470491100900408

Graham-Kevan, N. & Archer, J. (2009). Control tactics and partner violence in heterosexual relationships. *Evolution & Human Behavior,* 30, 445-452. doi: 10.1016/j.evolhumbehav.2009.06.007

Gray, J. (2007). *Black Mass: Apocalyptic Religion and the Death of Utopia.* Allen Lane.

Greenwood, A. K., Butler, P. C., White, R. B., DeMarco, U., Pearce, D. & Fernald, R. D. (2003). Multiple Corticosteroid Receptors in a Teleost Fish: Distinct Sequences, expression Patterns, and Transcriptional Activities. *Endocrinology,* 144(10), 4226-4236. doi: 10.1210/en.2003-0566

Gregory, S. W. (1990). Analysis of fundamental frequency reveals covariation in interview partners' speech. *Journal of Non-verbal Behavior,* 14(4), 237-251.

Gregory, S. W., Webster, S. & Huang, G. (1993). Voice pitch and amplitude convergence as a metric of quality in dyadic interviews. *Language & Communication,* 13(3), 195-217.

Gregory, S. W. & Webster, S. (1996). A nonverbal signal in voices of interview partners effectively predicts communication accommodation and social status. *Journal of Personal Social Psychology,* 70(6), 1231-1240. doi: 10.1.1.689.8611

Gregory, S. W., Dagan, K. & Webster, S. (1997). Evaluating the relation of vocal accommodation in conversation of partner's fundamental frequencies to perceptions of communication quality. *Journal of Non-verbal Behavior,* 21(1), 23-43. doi: 10.1023/A:1024995717773

Gregory, S. W. & Gallagher, T. J. (2002). Spectral analysis of candidates' non-verbal vocal communication: predicting US presidential election outcomes. *Social Psychology Quarterly,* 65(3), 298-308. doi: 10.2307/3090125

Hadjivasiliou, Z., Pomiankowski, A., Seymour, R. M. & Lane, N. (2012). Selection for mitonuclear co-adaptation could favour the evolution of two sexes. *Proceedings of the Royal Society: Biology,* 279(1734), 1865-1872. doi: 10.1098/rspb.2011.1871

Hakim, K. (2004). *Key Issues In Women's Work* (second edition). Glasshouse, London.

Hakim, K. (2003). *Models of the Family in Modern Societies: Ideals and Realities.* Ashgate.

Hakim, K. (2000). *Work-lifestyle Choices in the 21st Century: Preference theory.* Oxford University Press.

Harris, J. R. (1998, revised 2009). *The Nurture Assumption: Why Children Turn Out the Way They Do.* Free Press.

Harris, P. L. & Nuñez, M. (1996). Understanding of permission rules by preschool children. *Child Development,* 67, 1572-1591. doi: 10.1111/j.1467-8624.1996.tb01815.x

Harrison, P. W., Wright, A. E., Zimmer, F., Dean, R., Montgomery, S. H., Pointer, M. A. & Mank, J. E. (2015). Sexual selection drives evolution and rapid turnover of male gene expression. *PNAS USA,* 112(14), 4393-8. doi: 10.1073/pnas.1501339112

Hejll, A. (2001). Kön, makt och identitet: Erfarenheter från Rädda Barnens arbete mot könsstympning och forslag til framtida inriktning. Rädda Barnen. [p11]

Hemelrijk, C. (1999). An individual-oriented model of the emergence of despotic and egalitarian societies. *Procedures of the Royal Society, Biological Sciences,* 266(1417), 361. doi: 10.1098/rspb.1999.0646

Hemelrijk, C. K. (2000). *Social phenomena emerging by self-organisation in a competitive virtual world ('DomWorld')*. University of Zurich. http://www.ifi.uzh.ch/ailab/projects/collective/hemelrijkCELE2000.pdf doi: 10.1.1.32.7993

Hosken, F. P. (1993). *The Hosken Report: Genital and Sexual Mutilation of Females*. Fourth edition. Lexington, MA. Women's International Network, 39-40. doi: 10.2307/1159364

Hosken, F. P. (1989). *Female Genital Mutilation: Strategies for Eradication*. [Presentation to the First International Symposium on Circumcision, USA (http://www.nocirc.org).]

Hoyt, C. L. & Simon, S. (2011). Female Leaders: Injurious or Inspiring Role Models for Women? *Jepson School of Leadership Studies*. Paper 114. http://scholarship.richmond.edu/jepson-faculty-publications/114 doi: 10.1177/0361684310385216

Ireland, J. L. (1999). Bullying behaviors amongst male and female prisoners: A study of young offenders and adults. *Aggressive Behavior,* 25(3), 161-178. doi: 10.1002/(SICI)1098-2337(1999)25:3<161::AID-AB1>3.0.CO;2-#

Iriberri, N. & Rey-Biel, P. (2013). Let's (Not) Talk about Sex: Gender Awareness and Stereotype-Threat on Performance under Competition. Barcelona GSE Working Papers Series, Department of Economics, Universitat Pompeu Fabra. http://www.ed.ac.uk/polopoly_fs/1.106296!/fileManager/Jan2013Paper_Pedro_Rey_Biel.pdf

Ivanova-Stenzel, R. & Kübler, D. F. (2005). Courtesy and Idleness: Gender Differences in Team Work and Team Competition. IZA Discussion Paper no 1768. SSRNhttp://ssrn.com/abstract=825686

Iyer, P. L. (2009). Evolution of Sexual Dimorphism From Gametes To Ornaments. Dissertation, Dept of Biological Sciences, University of Stanford, USA. MI Number 32941.

Jezova, E., Skultetyova, I., Tokarev, D. I., Bakos, P. & Vigas, M. (1995). Vasopressin and oxytocin in stress. In Chrousos, G. P., McCarty, R., Pacak, K., Cizza, G., Sternberg, E., Gold, P. W. & Kvetnansky, R. (eds) Stress: Basic mechanisms and clinical mechanisms and clinical implications, 771, 192-203. New York: Annals of the New York Academy of Sciences. doi: 10.1111/j.1749-6632.1995.tb44681.x

Jezova, D., Jurankova, E., Mosnarova, A., Kriska, M. & Skultetyova, I. (1996). Neuroendocrine response during stress with relation to gender differences. *Acta Neurobiologae Experimentalis,* 56, 779-785.

Johnson, K. & Burley, N. T. (1998). Mating tactics and mating systems of birds. Ornithological Monographs, 49. Avian Reproductive Tactics: Female and Male Perspectives. University of California Press. 21-60. doi: 10.2307/40166717

Juster, R. P. & Lupien, S. J. (2012). Sex and gender in stress research: the metamorphosis of a field, In *What a Difference Sex and Gender Make: A Gender, Sex and Health Research Casebook*. Canadian Institute of Health Research.

Kalma, A. (1991). Hierarchisation and dominance at first glance. *European Journal of Social Psychology,* 21(2), 165-181. doi: 10.1002/ejsp.2420210206

Kappeler, P. M. (1993). Female dominance in primates and other mammals, in *Perspectives in Ethology, Behavior and Evolution* (ed Bateson PPG, Klopfer PH, & Thompson NS), 10, 143-158. New York, Plenum.

Keller, L. (1999). *Levels of Selection in Evolution.* Princeton University Press.

Kempenaers, B., Verheyen, G. R., Broeck, M. V., Burke, T., Broeckhoven, C. V. & Dhonth, A. A. (1992). Extra-pair paternity results from female preference for high-quality males in the blue tit. *Nature,* 357, 494-496. doi: 10.1038/357494a0

Kimchi, T., Xu, J. & Dulac, C. (2007). A functional circuit underlying male sexual behaviour in the female mouse brain. *Nature,* 448(7157), 1009-14. doi:10.1038/nature06089

Kinias, A. (2010). *History of the veil: part one: veil in the ancient world.* http://alexandrakinias.wordpress.com/2010/06/27/history-of-the-veil-part-one-veil-in-the-ancient-world/

Kleinbaum, A. M., Stuart, T. E. & Tushman, M. L. (2011). *Discretion Within the Constraints of Opportunity: Gender Homophily and Structure in a Formal Organization.* Working Paper, Harvard Business School. http://www.hbs.edu/faculty/Publication%20Files/12-050.pdf

Kling, K. C., Noftle, E. E. & Robins, R. W. (2013). Why do standardized tests under-predict women's academic performance? The role of conscientiousness. *Social Psychological and Personality Science,* 4(5), 600-606. doi:10.1177/1948550612469038

Ko, D. (2008). *Cinderella's Sisters: A Revisionist History of Footbinding.* University of California Press.

Kokko, H. & Morrell, L. J. (2005). Mate guarding, male attractiveness, and paternity under social monogamy. *Behavioral Ecology,* 16, 724-731. doi: 10.1093/beheco/ari050

Koroma, J. M. (2002). *Female Genital Mutilation In The Gambia: A Desk Review.* National Women's Bureau Office of the Vice President, The Gambia. [pp12-13] http://www.unicef.org/wcaro/wcaro_gambia_FGM_Desk_Review.pdf

Korotayev, A. (2003). An Apologia of George Peter Murdock. Division of Labor by Gender and Postmarital Residence in Cross-Cultural Perspective: A Reconsideration. *World Cross-Cultural Research,* 37(4), 335-372. doi: 10.1177/1069397103253685

Lanctot, R. B. & Best, L. B. (2000). Comparison of methods for determining dominance rank in male and female prairie voles. *Journal of Mammalogy,* 81(3), 734-745. doi: 10.1644/1545-1542(2000)081<0734:COMFDD>2.3.CO;2

Landry, N. E. R. (2008). *The Mean Girl Motive: Negotiating Power and Femininity.* Fernwood Publishing.

Lane, N. (2009). Why sex is worth losing your head for. *New Scientist,* 13 June. 40-43. http://www.nick-lane.net/OriginofSex.pdf

Langhinrichsen-Rohling, J., Selwyn, C. & Rohling, M. L. (2012). Rates of bidirectional versus unidirectional intimate partner violence across samples, sexual orientations, and race/ethnicities: a comprehensive review. *Partner Abuse,* 3(2), 199-230(32). doi: 10.1891/1946-6560.3.2.199

Lee, J. & Harley, V. R. (2012). The male fight-flight response: A result of SRY regulation of catecholamines? *BioEssays,* 34(6), 454-457. doi: 10.1002/bies.201100159

Lee, S. Y., Kesebir, S. & Pillutla, M. M. (2016). Gender differences in response to competition with same-gender co-workers: a relational perspective. *Journal of Personality and Social Psychology,* 110(6), 869-886. doi: 10.1037/pspi0000051

Lessells, C. M. (1999). Sexual conflict in animals. P97 in (Keller, L. ed) *Levels of Selection in Evolution.* Monographs in Behavior and Ecology. Princeton University Press, NJ.

Levy, H. S. (1992). *The Lotus Lovers: The Complete History of the Curious Erotic Custom of Footbinding in China.* Buffalo NY. Prometheus Books.

Lezalová-Piálková, R. (2010). Molecular evidence for extra-pair paternity and intra-specific brood parasitism in the black-headed gull. *Journal of Ornithology,* 152(2), 291-295. doi: 10.1007/s10336-010-0581-1

Lie, G., Schilit, R., Bush, R., Montagne, M. & Reyes L. (1991) Lesbians in currently aggressive relationships: how frequently do they report aggressive past relationships? *Violence and Victims,* 6, 121-135.

Lighthall, N. R., Sakaki, M., Vasunilashorn, S., Nga, L., Somayajula, S., Chen, E. Y., Samii, N. & Mather, M. (2012). Gender differences in reward-related decision processing under stress. *Social Cognitive & Affective Neuroscience,* 7(4), 476-484. doi: 10.1093/scan/nsr026

Lindenlaub, I. & Prummer, A. (2013). More versus Closer Friends: How Gender Shapes Social Networks and their Effects on Performance. http://www2.warwick.ac.uk/fac/soc/economics/events/seminars-schedule/conferences/ctn/prummer_paper.pdf

Lindner, M. (2008). *The Social Dimension of Female Genital Cutting (FGC): The Case of Harari.* Addis Ababa University, School of Graduate Studies, The Gambia. http://etd.aau.edu.et/bitstream/123456789/1952/2/Mandy%20Lindner.pdf

Lion, S., Jansen, V. A. A. & Day, T. (2011). Evolution in structured populations: Beyond the kin versus group debate. *Trends in Ecology and Evolution,* 26(4), 193. doi: 10.1016/j.tree.2011.01.006

Long, T. A. F., Pischedda, A., Stewart, A.D., Rice, W. R. (2009). A cost of sexual attractiveness to high-fitness females. *PLoS Biology,* 7(12), e1000254. doi: 10.1371/journal.pbio.1000254

Lovallo, W. R., Enoch, M. A., Acheson, A., Cohoon, A. J., Sorocco, K. H., Hodgkinson, C. A., Vincent, A.S., Glahn, D. C. & Goldman, D. (2015). Cortisol Stress Response in Men and Women Modulated Differentially by the Mu-Opioid Receptor Gene. *Neuropsychopharmacology,* 40(11), 2546-2554. doi: 10.1038/npp.2015.101

Lumley, A., Michalczyk, L., Kitson, J., Spurgin, L., Morrison, C., Godwin, J., Dickinson, M., Martin, O., Emerson, B., Chapman, T. & Gage, M. (2015). Sexual selection protects against extinction. *Nature,* 522 (7557), 470-473. doi: 10.1038/nature14419

Lumpkin, S. (1983). Female manipulation of male avoidance of cuckoldry behavior in the ring dove. In *Social Behavior* (Ed Wasser SK), 91-112. Academic Press, New York.

Mace, R. & Sear, R. (2005). Are humans co-operative breeders? In: Voland E, Chasoitis A & Schiefenhoevel W, editors. *Grandmotherhood: The Evolutionary Significance of the Second Half of Female Life*. Piscataway: Rutgers University Press. [pp143-15]

Mace, R. & Sear, R. (2008). Who keeps children alive? A review of the effects of kin on child survival. *Evolution and Human Behavior,* 29(1), 1-18. doi: 10.1016/j.evolhumbehav.2007.10.001

Mackie, G. (1996). Ending Footbinding and Infibulation: A Convention Account. *American Sociological Review,* 61(6), 999-1017. [p1001] doi: 10.2307/2096305

Maddux, W. & Brewer, M. (2005). Gender differences in the relational and collective bases for trust. *Group Processes Intergroup Relations,* 8(2), 159-171. doi: 10.1177/1368430205051065

Magdol, L., Moffitt, T. E., Caspi, A., Fagan, J. & Silva, P. A. (1997). Gender differences in partner violence in a birth cohort of 21 year olds: Bridging the gap between clinical and epidemiological approaches. *Journal of Consulting and Clinical Psychology,* 65, 68-78. doi: 10.1037/0022-006X.65.1.68

Mallet, M.A., Bouchard, J.M., Kimber, C.M. & Chippindale, A.K. (2011). Experimental mutation-accumulation on the X chromosome of Drosophila melanogaster reveals stronger selection on males than females. *BMC Evolutionary Biology,* 11(1), 156. doi: 10.1186/1471-2148-11-156

Manson, J.H. (1997). Primate Consortships: A Critical Review. *Current Anthropology,* 38(3), 353-374. doi: 10.1086/204623

Marcinkowska, U. M., Moore, F.R. & Rantala, M.J. (2013). An experimental test of the Westermarck effect: sex differences in inbreeding avoidance. *Behavioral Ecology,* 24(4), 842-845. doi: 10.1093/beheco/art028

Marmot, M.G., Smith, G.D., Stansfeld, S., Patel, C., North, F., Head, J., White, I., Brunner, E. & Feeney, A. (1991). Health inequalities among British civil servants: the Whitehall II study. *The Lancet,* 337(8754), 1387-1393. doi:10.1016/0140-6736(91)93068-K

Marmot, M. G. (2004). *Status Syndrome: How Social Standing Affects our Health and Longevity*. Bloomsbury.

Martin, C. L., Kornienko, O., Schaefer, D. R., Hanish, L. D., Fabes, R. A. & Goble, P. (2013). The Role of Sex of Peers and Gender-Typed Activities in Young Children's Peer Affiliative Networks: A Longitudinal Analysis of Selection and Influence. *Child Development,* 84, 921-937. doi: 10.1111/cdev.12032

Mavin, S. & Bryans, P. (2003). Women's place in organization: the role of female misogyny. Paper presented at the Third International Gender, Work and Organization Conference, Keele, UK.

Mavin, S. & Lockwood, A. (2004). Sisterhood and solidarity vs queen bees and female misogyny: A future for women in management? British Academy of Management Conference, St Andrews.

Maynard Smith, J. & Szathmary, E. (1995). *The Major Transitions in Evolution*. Oxford University Press.

Mazur, A., Susman, E. J. & Edelbrock, S. (1997). Sex differences in testosterone response to a video game competition. *Evolution and Human behaviour*, 18, 317-326. doi: 10.1016/S1090-5138(97)00013-5

McCarthy, M. M. (1995). Estrogen modulation of oxytocin and its relation to behavior. In Ivell, R. & Russell, J. (eds) Oxytocin: Cellular and Molecular Approaches in Medicine and Research, 235-242. New York: Plenum Polymorphism OPRM1 A118G.

McGuigan, K., Petfield, D. & Blows, M. W. (2011). Reducing mutation load through sexual selection on males. *Evolution*, 65(10), 2816-2829. doi: 10.1111/j.1558-5646.2011.01346.x

Mehl, B. & Buchner, A. (2008). No enhanced memory for faces of cheaters. *Evolution & Human Behavior*, 29, 35-41. doi: 10.1016/j.evolhumbehav.2007.08.001

Mehta, C. M. & Strough, J. (2009). Sex segregation in friendships and normative contexts across the life span. *Developmental Review*, 29, 201-220. doi: 10.1016/j.dr.2009.06.001

Minni, A. M., de Medeiros, G. F., Helbling, J. C., Duittoz, A., Marissal-Arvy, N., Foury, A. & Moisan, M. P. (2014). Role of corticosteroid binding globulin in emotional reactivity sex differences in mice. *Psychoneuroendocrinology*, 50, 252-263. doi: 10.1016/j.psyneuen.2014.07.029

Mirrlees-Black, C., Budd, T., Partridge, S. & Mayhew, P. (1998). *The 1998 British crime survey*. Government Statistical Service, Home Office. London.

Moir, A. & Moir, W. (1998). *Why Men Don't Iron: The Real Science of Gender Studies*. Harper Collins.

Molm, L. D. (1986). Gender, power, and legitimation: A test of three theories. *American Journal of Sociology*, 91(6), 1356-1386. doi: 10.1086/228425

Morse, B. J. (1995). Beyond the Conflict Tactics Scale: Assessing gender differences in partner violence. *Violence & Victims*, 4, 251-271.

Moser, K., Pugh, H. & Goldblatt, P. (1990). Inequalities in women's health in England and Wales: mortality among married women according to social circumstances, employment characteristics and life cycle stage. *Genus*, 46(3-4), 71-84.

Moxon, S. P. (2015a). Stress mechanism is sex-specific: Female amelioration or escape from stress to avoid compromising reproduction contrasts with male utilisation or in effect manufacture of stress to fulfil male 'genetic filter' function. *New Male Studies*, 4(3), 50-62. http://www.newmalestudies.com/OJS/index.php/nms/article/view/194/222

Moxon, S. P. (2015b). Competitiveness is profoundly sex-differential, consistent with being biologically based and within-, not between-sex. *New Male Studies*, 4(2), 39-51. http://www.newmalestudies.com/OJS/index.php/nms/article/view/186

Moxon, S. P. (2014). Partner violence as female-specific in aetiology. *New Male Studies,* 3(3), 69-92. http://www.newmalestudies.com/OJS/index.php/nms/article/view/149

Moxon, S. P. (2014). From DNA repair to social minds: The root of sex-dichotomous psychology and behaviour. [Presentation for the conference 'From DNA To Social Minds', University of York, June/July 2014.]

Moxon, S. P. (2014). Demographic transition as caused by biological effects of social dislocation: adaptive reproductive-suppression triggered by 'crowding' stress of males transmitted epigenetically to female offspring multi-generationally; plus out-breeding fertility depression through genetic incompatibilities. [Accepted for conference presentation.]

Moxon, S. P. (2013). Human pair-bonding as primarily a service to the female (in excluding other males of lower (but not higher) mate-value, and a buffer against her own age-related mate-value decline). *New Male Studies,* 2(2), 24-38. http://newmalestudies.com/OJS/index.php/nms/article/view/71

Moxon, S. P. (2012). The origin of the sexual divide in the 'genetic filter' function: Male disadvantage and why it is not perceived. *New Male Studies,* 1(3), 96-12. http://newmalestudies.com/OJS/index.php/nms/article/view/47

Moxon, S. P. (2012). The Reasons Why Women Won't Match Men in the Workplace Irrespective of Whatever Action is Taken. [Submission to the inquiry 'Women in the Workplace', for The Business, Innovation and Skills Select Committee, House of Commons.] http://www.publications.parliament.uk/pa/cm201213/cmselect/cmbis/writev/womeninworkplace/m22.htmo

Moxon, S. P. (2011). Beyond staged retreat behind virtual 'gender paradigm' barricades: The rise and fall of the misrepresentation of partner-violence and its eclipse by an understanding of 'mate-guarding'. *Journal of Aggression, Conflict & Peace Research,* 3(1), 45-54. http://www.emeraldinsight.com/journals.htm?articleid=1932380&show=html doi: 10.5042/jacpr.2011.0021

Moxon, S. P. (2010). Culture is biology: Why we cannot 'transcend' our genes – or ourselves. *Politics & Culture* (journal). [On-line symposium, 'How Is Culture Biological?'] http://www.politicsandculture.org/2010/04/29/symposium-on-the-question-how-is-culture-biological-six-essays-and-discussions-essay-1-by-steve-moxon-culture-is-biology-why-we-cannot-transcend-our-genes%E2%80%94or-ourselves/

Moxon, S. P. (2009). Dominance as adaptive stressing and ranking of males, serving to allocate reproduction by differential self-suppressed fertility: Towards a fully biological understanding of social systems. *Medical Hypotheses,* 73(1), 5-14. http://www.medical-hypotheses.com/article/S0306-9877(09)00145-5/abstract doi: 10.1016/j.mehy.2009.02.011

Moxon, S. P. (2008). *The Woman Racket: The New Science Explaining How the Sexes Relate at Work, at Play and in Society.* Imprint Academic.

Murdock, G. P. (1967). *Ethnographic Atlas: A Summary*. The University of Pittsburgh Press.

Naddesen, K. (2000). A Profile of Female Genital Mutilation and Human Rights: Towards outlawing the Practice. *Alternation,* 7(2). 170-192. [p171] http://reference.sabinet.co.za/webx/access/journal_archive/10231757/230.pdf

Nemet-Nejat, K. R. (1998). *Daily Life in Ancient Mesopotamia*. Westport, CT Greenwood Press.

Kitchen, D. M. & Packer, C. (1999). Complexity in vertebrate societies. In Keller, L. (ed) (1999). *Levels of Selection in Evolution*. Princeton University Press.

Niederle, M. (2015). Gender, in *Handbook of Experimental Economics* Vol 2, ed Kagel, J., Roth, A. E. & Nielson, P. I. (2009). *A History of the Veil in Mesopotamia and Persia*. http://suite101.com/article/a-history-of-the-veil-in-mesopotamia-and-persia-a183203

Noble, D. (2008). *The Music of Life: Biology Beyond Genes*. Oxford University Press.

Norscia, I. & Borgognini-Tarli, S. M. (2008). Ranging behavior and possible correlates of pair-living in South-eastern Avahis (Madagascar) *International Journal of Primatology,* 29(1), 153-171. doi: 10.1007/s10764-007-9219-4

Novak, M. A., Tarnita, C. E. & Wilson, E. O. (2010). The evolution of eusociality. *Nature,* 466, 1057-1062. doi: 10.1038/nature09205

Nunney, L. (1999). Lineage selection: natural selection for long-term benefit. In Keller (ed) *Levels of Selection in Evolution,* 238-252.

Oda, R. (1997). Biased face recognition in the Prisoner's Dilemma Game. *Evolution & Human Behavior,* 18(5), 309-315.

Okasha, S. (2008). *Evolution and the Levels of Selection*. Oxford University Press.

Omark, R. D., Omark, M. V. & Edelman, M. S. (1975). Formation of dominance hierarchies in young children: Action and perception. In Williams, T. R. (ed) *Psychological anthropology*. Mouton Publishers, Paris.

Onojeharho, J. E. & Bloom, L. (1986). Inmate subculture in a Nigerian prison. *The Newspaper of Psychology,* 120(5), 421-432. doi: 10.1080/00223980.1986.9915473

ONS (Office for National Statistics). (2014). Crime Survey for England and Wales. Statistical Bulletin: Focus on: Violent Crime and Sexual Offences 2012/13. Appendix table 4.22.

Onyishi, I. E., Prokop, P., Okafor, C. O. & Pham, M. N. (2016). Female Genital Cutting Restricts Sociosexuality Among the Igbo People of Southeast Nigeria. *Evolutionary Psychology,* 14(2). doi: 10.1177/1474704916648784

Paland, S. & Lynch, M. (2006). Transitions to asexuality result in excess amino acid substitutions. *Science,* 311, 990-992. doi: 10.1126/science.1118152

Palchykov, V., Kaski, K., Kertesz, J., Barabasi, A-L. & Dunbar, R. I. M. (2012). Sex differences in intimate relationships. *Scientific Reports,* 2(370). doi: 10.1038/srep00370

Partridge, L. & Fowler, K. (1990). Non-mating costs of exposure to males in female Drosophila melanogaster. *Journal of Insect Physiology,* 36, 419-425. doi: 10.1016/0022-1910(90)90059-O

Ping, W. (2000). *Aching for Beauty: Footbinding in China.* University of Minnesota Press. [p4]

Pinker, S. (2003). *The Blank Slate: The Modern Denial of Human Nature.* Penguin.

Pinker, S. (1997). *How the Mind Works.* Norton & Co.

Plomin, R. & Daniels, D. (1987). Why are children in the same family so different from one another? *Behavioral and Brain Sciences,* 10(1). 1-16. doi: 10.1093/ije/dyq148

Popielarz, P. A. (1999). (In)Voluntary Association: A Multilevel Analysis of Gender Segregation in Voluntary Organizations. *Gender & Society,* 13(2), 234-250. doi: 10.1177/089124399013002005

Population Council. (1999). *Strengthening Reproductive Health Services in Africa through Operations Research.* Africa Operations Research and Technical Assistance Project II, Final Report. [p93] http://pdf.usaid.gov/pdf_docs/Pdabs735.pdf

Population Reference Bureau. (2001). *La Juventude del Mundo 2000.* Washington. [p24]

Powers, S. T., Penn, A. S. & Watson, R. A. (2011). The concurrent evolution of cooperation and the population structures that support it. *Evolution,* 65(6). 1527-1543. doi: 10.1111/j.1558-5646.2011.01250.x

Priya, S. (2007). "Nahid Toubia". *The Lancet,* 369(9564), 819. doi: 0.1016/S0140-6736(07)60394-8

Raghubir, P. & Valenzuela, A. (2009). Male-Female Dynamics in Groups: A Field Study of The Weakest Link. *Small Group Research,* XX(X), 1-30. doi: 10.1177/1046496409352509

Reeve, S. D., Kelly, K. M., & Welling, L. L. M. (2016). Transitory environmental stress alters sexual strategies & sexually dimorphic mate preferences. *Evolutionary Psychological Science,* 2(2), 101-113. doi: 10.1007/s40806-015-0040-6

Riffkin, R. (2014). *Americans Still Prefer a Male Boss to a Female Boss. Women are more likely than men to prefer a female boss.* Gallup. http://www.gallup.com/poll/178484/americans-prefer-male-boss-female-boss.aspx

Rose, J.A. & Rudolph, K. D. (2011). A Review of Sex Differences in Peer Relationship Processes: Potential Trade-offs for the Emotional and Behavioral Development of Girls and Boys. *Psychological Bulletin,* 132(1), 98-131. doi: 10.1037/0033-2909.132.1.98

Roughgarden, J. & Iyer, P. (2011). Contact, not conflict, causes the evolution of anisogamy pp 96-110, in Togashi & Cox (ed), *The Evolution of Anisogamy: A Fundamental Phenomenon Underlying Sexual Selection.*

Roze, D. & Otto, S. P. (2012). Differential Selection Between the Sexes and Selection for Sex. *Evolution,* 66(2), 558-574. doi: 10.1111/j.1558-5646.2011.01459.x

Rubin, K. H. & Coplan, R. J. (1993). Peer relationships in childhood. In Bornstein, M. & Lamb, M. (eds) *Developmental psychology: an advanced textbook.*

Rye, S. (2002). *Circumcision in Urban Ethiopia: Practices, Discourses and Contexts.* Doctoral dissertation, Department of Anthropology, University of Oslo. [pp189-193]

Sacker, A., Firth, D., Fitzpatrick, R., Lynch, K. & Bartley, M. (2000). Comparing health inequality in men and women: prospective study of mortality. *British Medical Journal,* 320(7245), 1303-1307. doi: 10.1136/bmj.320.7245.1303

Sagarin, B. J., Martin, A. L., Coutinho, S. A., Edlund, J. E., Patel, L., Zengel, B. & Skowronski, J. J. (2012). Sex differences in jealousy: a meta-analytic examination. *Evolution & Human Behavior,* 33(6), 595-614. doi: 10.1016/j.evolhumbehav.2012.02.006

Sæverås, E. F. (2002). Accounts of Kenyan consultants on assignment for NCA/Somalia programme. In (2003). *Female Genital Mutilation: Understanding the issues.* Norwegian Church Aid.

Scelza, B. A. (2011). Female choice and extra-pair paternity in a traditional human population. *Biology Letters,* 237(6), 889-891. doi: 10.1098/rsbl.2011.0478

Sebanc, A. M., Pierce, S. L., Cheatham, C. L. & Gunnar, M. R. (2003). Gendered Social Worlds in Preschool: Dominance, Peer Acceptance and Assertive Social Skills in Boys' and Girls' Peer Groups. *Social Development,* 12(1), 91-106. doi: 10.1111/1467-9507.00223

Segal, M., Peck, J., Vega-Lahr, N. & Field, T. M. (1987). A medieval kingdom: leader-follower styles of preschool play. *Journal of Applied Developmental Psychology,* 8(1), 79-95. doi:10.1016/0193-3973(87)90022-0

Shattuck, K., Dillon, L., Nowak, N., Weisfeld, G., Weisfeld, C., Imamoðlu, O., Butovskaya, M. & Shen, J. (2012). When the cat's away, the spouse will play: A cross-cultural examination of mate-guarding in married couples. [Presentation to the ISHE XXI biennial international conference on human ethology, Vienna.]

Shweder, R. A. (2000). What about 'female genital mutilation'? And why understanding culture matters in the first place? *Daedalus,* 129(4), 209-232. [p222]

Siller, S. (2001). Sexual selection and the maintenance of sex. *Nature,* 411, 689-692. doi:10.1038/35079590

Simmons, R. (2011, 2002). *Odd Girl Out: The Hidden Culture Of Aggression in Girls.* Mariner Books.

Singh, R. S. & Artieri, C. G. (2010). Male Sex Drive and the Maintenance of Sex: Evidence from Drosophila. *Journal of Heredity,* 101(1), S100-106. doi: 10.1093/jhered/esq006

Sohn, K. (2016). Men's revealed preferences regarding women's ages: evidence from prostitution. *Evolution & Human Behavior,* 37(4), 272-280. doi: 10.1016/j.evolhumbehav.2016.01.002

Sokhi, D. S., Hunter, M. D. & Wilkinson, I. D. (2005). Male and female voices activate distinct regions in the male brain. *Neuroimage,* 27(3). 572-578. doi: 10.1016/j.neuroimage.2005.04.023

Sordaz, S. & Luna, B. (2012). Sex differences in physiological reactivity to acute psychosocial stress in adolescence. *Psychoneuroendocrinology,* 37(8), 1135-1157. doi: 10.1016/j.psyneuen.2012.01.002

Sorrells, M. et al (2007). Fine-Touch Pressure Thresholds in the Adult Penis. *British Journal of Urology International,* 99, 864-869. doi: 10.1111/j.1464-410X.2006.06685.x

Sterrenburg, L. (2012). The stress response of forebrain and midbrain regions: neuropeptides, sex-specificity and epigenetics, 93, FCDC series. UB Nijbergen.

Stets, J. E. & Straus, M.A. (1990). Gender differences in reporting of marital violence and its medical and psychological consequences. In Straus & Gelles (eds) *Physical violence in American families 1,* 151-166. Transaction Publishers.

Stoet, G. & Geary, D. C. (2012). Can Stereotype Threat Explain the Gender Gap in Mathematics Performance and Achievement? *Review of General Psychology,* 16(1), 93-102. doi: http://dx.doi.org/10.1037/a0026617

Stowers, L., Holy, T. E., Meister, M., Dulac, C. & Koentges, G. (2002). Loss of sex discrimination and male-male aggression in mice deficient for TRP2. *Science,* 295(559), 1493-1450. doi: 10.1126/science.1069259

Stroud, L. R., Salovey, P. & Epel, E. S. (2002). Sex differences in adrenocortical responses to achievement and interpersonal stress. *Biological Psychiatry,* 54(2), 318-327. doi: : 10.1016/S0006-3223(02)01333-1

Sutter, M. & Rutzler, D. (2010). Gender differences in competition emerge early in life: Three-year old girls compete as much as boys, but older girls don't. University of Innsbruck. Mimeo.

Szell, M. & Thurner, S. (2013). How women organize social networks different from men. *Scientific Reports,* 3, 1214. http://www.nature.com/srep/2013/130207/srep01214/full/srep01214.html?WT.ec_id=SREP-20130212 doi: 10.1038/srep0121

Szepsenwol, O., Mikulincer, M. & Birnbaum, G. E. (2013). Misguided attraction: The contribution of normative and individual-differences components of the sexual system to mating preferences. *Journal of Research in Personality,* 47(3), 196-200. doi: 10.1016/j.jrp.2013.01.002

Tarin, J. J. & Gomez-Piquer, V. (2002). Do women have a hidden heat period? *Human Reproduction,* 17(9), 2243-2248. doi: 10.1093/humrep/17.9.224

Taylor, J., Lockwood, A. P. & Taylor, A. J. (1996). The Prepuce: Specialized Mucosa of the Penis and Its Loss to Circumcision. *British Journal of Urology International,* 77(2), 291-295. doi: 10.1046/j.1464-410X.1996.85023.x

Taylor, S.E., Klein, L., Lewis, B. P., Gruenewald, T. L., Gurung, R. R. & Updegraff, J. A. (2000). Biobehavioral responses to stress in females: Tend-and-befriend, not fight-or-flight. *Psychological Review,* 107, 411-429. doi: 10.1037/0033-295X.107.3.411

Thompson, G. (2010). *Domestic violence statistics*. House of Commons Library SN/SG/950. http://www.parliament.uk/briefing-papers/SN00950.pdf

Thompson, R. R., George, K., Walton, J. C., Orr, S. P. & Benson, J. (2005). Sex-specific influences of vasopressin on human social communication. *PNAS,* 103(20), 7889-7894. doi: 10.1073/pnas.0600406103

Thornhill, R. & Gangestad, S. W. (2008). *The Evolutionary Biology of Human Female Sexuality.* Oxford University Press.

Tognetti, A., Dubois, D., Faurie, C. & Willinger, M. (2016). *Are co-operative men showing off? Contributions to a public good are larger under sexual competition.* Presentations at the Stirling biennial conference of the International Society for Human Ethology (ISHE) and the London annual conference of the European Human Behaviour & Evolution Association (EHBEA). Mimeo.

Toufexis, D., Rivarola, M. A., Lara, H. & Viau, V. (2013). Stress and the Reproductive Axis. *Journal of Neuroendocrinology,* 26(9), 573-586. doi: 10.1111/jne.12179

Tunç, B., Solmaz, B., Parker, D., Satterthwaite, T. D., Elliott, M. A., Calkins, M.E., Ruparel, K., Gur, R. E., Gur, R. C. & Verma, R. (2016). Establishing a link between sex-related differences in the structural connectome and behaviour. *Philosophical Transactions of the Royal Society B: Biological Sciences,* 371(1688). doi: 10.1098/rstb.2015.0111

Turkheimer, E. (2000). Three laws of behavior genetics and what they mean. *Current Directions in Psychological Science,* 9(5), 160-165. doi: 10.1111/1467-8721.00084

Turkheimer, E. & Waldron, M. C. (2000). Non-shared environment: A theoretical, methodological, and quantitative review. *Psychological Bulletin,* 126, 78-108. doi: 10.1037/0033-2909.126.1.78

UNFPA. (2007). *Creating a Safe Haven and a Better Future for Maasai Girls Escaping Violence.* http://www.unfpa.org/news/safe-haven-girls-escaping-harm-kenya

Urberg, K. A. (1992). Locus of peer influence: Social crowd and best friend. *Journal of Youth and Adolescence,* 21(4), 439-450. doi: 10.1007/BF01537896

Urberg, K. A., Degirmencioglu, S. M., Tolson, J. M. & Halliday-Scher, K. D. (1995). The structure of adolescent peer networks. *Developmental Psychology,* 31(4), 540-547. doi: 10.1037//0012-1649.31.4.540

Urberg, K. A., Degirmenciogl, S. M., Tolson, J. M. & Halliday-Scher, K. D. (2000). Adolescent social crowds: Measurement and relationship to friendships. *Journal of Adolescent Research,* 15(4), 427-445. doi: 10.1177/0743558400154001

Uvnas-Moberg, K. (1997). Oxytocin linked anti-stress effects: The relaxation and growth response. *Acta Psychologica Scandinavica,* 640 (supplement), 38-42.

Van den Berg, W. E., Lamballais, S. & Kushner, S. A. (2015). Sex-specific mechanism of social hierarchy in mice. *Neuropsychopharmacology,* 40(6),1364-1372. doi: 10.1038/npp.2014.319

Van Lier, J., Revlin, R. & De Neys, W. (2013). Detecting Cheaters without Thinking: Testing the Automaticity of the Cheater Detection Module. *PLoS ONE,* 8(1), e53827. doi: 10.1371/journal.pone.0053827

Vogel, D.L., Murphy, M. J., Werner-Wilson, R. J., Cutrona, C. E. & Seeman, J. (2007). Sex differences in the use of demand and withdraw behavior in marriage. *Journal of Counseling Psychology,* 54(2). 165-177. doi: 10.1037/0022-0167.54.2.165

Wang, J., Korczykowski, M., Rao, H., Fan, Y., Pluta, J., Gurl, R. C., McEwan, B. S. & Detre, J. A. (2007). Gender difference in neural response to psychological stress. *Social, Cognitive & Affective Neuroscience,* 2(3), 227-239. doi: 10.1093/scan/nsm018

Walston, F., David, A. S. & Charlton, B. G. (1998). Sex differences in the content of persecutory delusions: a reflection of hostile threats in the ancestral environment? *Evolution and Human behaviour,* 19(4), 257-260. doi: 10.1016/S1090-5138(98)00010-5

Wang, Y., Ma, Y., Hu, J., Cheng, W., Jiang, H., Zhang, X., Li, M., Ren, J. & Li, X. (2015). Prenatal chronic mild stress induces depression-like behavior and sex-specific changes in regional glutamate receptor expression patterns in adult rats. *Neuroscience,* 363(74), 1873-7544. doi: 10.1016/j.neuroscience.2015.06.008

Ward, D. A. & Kassebaum, G. G. (1965). *Women's Prison: Sex and Social Structure.* Aldine Publishing Co, Chicago.

Webster, R. (1995, 2005). *Why Freud Was Wrong: Sin, Science and Psychoanalysis.* Oxford: The Orwell Press.

West-Eberhard, M. J. (2005). The maintenance of sex as a developmental trap due to sexual selection. *Quarterly Review of Biology,* 80(1), 47-53. doi: 10.1086/431024

Whitlock, M. C. & Agrawal, A. F. (2009). Purging the genome with sexual selection: reducing mutation Load through selection on males. *Evolution,* 63(3), 569-582. doi: 10.1111/j.1558-5646.2008.00558.x

Whitaker, D. J., Haileyesus, T., Swahn, M. & Saltzman, L. S. (2007). Differences in frequency of violence and reported injury between relationships with reciprocal and non-reciprocal intimate partner violence. *American Journal of Public Health,* 97(5), 941-947. doi: 10.2105/AJPH.2005.079020

Whitehall I study. (1967-). Department of Epidemiology & Public Health, University College of London. http://www.workhealth.org/projects/pwhitew.html

Whitehall II study. (1985-). Department of Epidemiology & Public Health, University College of London. http://www.ucl.ac.uk/whitehall II

Wilder. J. A., Mobasher, Z. & Hammer, M. F. (2004). Genetic evidence for unequal effective population sizes of human females and males. *Molecular Biology & Evolution,* 21(11), 2047-2057. doi: 10.1093/molbev/msh214

Williams, J. H., Van Dorn, R. A., Hawkins, J. D., Abbott, R. & Catalano, R. F. (2001). Correlates contributing to involvement in violent behaviors among young adults. *Violence and Victims,* 16, 371-388.

Wilson, E. O. (1978). *On Human Nature.* Penguin.

Winking, J. (2006). Are men really that bad as fathers? The role of men's investments. *Biodemography and Social Biology,* 53(1-2), 100-115. doi: 10.1080/19485565.2006.9989119

Wiseman, R. (2009, 2002). *Queen Bees & Wannabes: Helping Your Daughter to Survive Cliques, Gossip, Boyfriends, and Other Realities of Adolescence.* Three Rivers Press.

Worku Zerai / Norwegian Church Aid (2003) *A Study on Female Genital Mutilation in Eritrea.* NCA/NORAD, Asmara. [p17]

Wright, A. E. & Mank, J. E. (2013). The scope and strength of sex-specific selection in genome evolution. *Journal of Evolutionary Biology,* 26(9), 1841-1853. doi: 10.1111/jeb.12201

Yamagishi, T. & Mifune, N. (2009). Social exchange and solidarity: In-group love or out-group hate? *Evolution & Human Behavior,* 30(4), 229-237. doi: 10.1016/j.evolhumbehav.2009.02.004

Yuan, Q., Song, Y., Yang, C-H., Jan, L. Y. & Jan, Y. N .(2014). Female contact modulates male aggression via a sexually dimorphic GABAergic circuit in Drosophila. *Nature Neuroscience,* 17(1), 81-88. doi:10.1038/nn.3581

Zolotova, J. & Brune, M. (2006). Persecutory delusions: reminiscence of ancestral hostile threats? *Evolution & Human Behavior,* 27(3), 185-192. doi: 10.1016/j.evolhumbehav.2005.08.001

# Notes pages

# Notes pages

# NOTES PAGES

# Notes pages

# NOTES PAGES